The

Death of

Literature

The Death of Literature

ALVIN KERNAN

YALE UNIVERSITY PRESS NEW HAVEN & LONDON

Designed by Nancy Ovedovitz. Set in Bodoni type by Brevis Press, Bethany, Connecticut. Printed in the United States of America by Vail-Ballou Press, Binghamton, New York.

Library of Congress Cataloging-in-Publication Data

Kernan, Alvin B.

The death of literature / Alvin Kernan.

    p.   cm.

Includes bibliographical references.

ISBN 0-300-04783-5 (cloth)

        0-300-05238-3 (pbk.)

1. Postmodernism (Literature)   2. Criticism.   I. Title.

PN98.P67K47   1990

801'.95'09045—dc20   90-31208

                                                                      CIP

The paper in this book meets the guidelines for permanence and durability of the Committee on Production Guidelines for Book Longevity of the Council on Library Resources.

10   9   8   7   6   5   4   3   2

For A. Bartlett Giamatti
Former Student and Colleague,
Always Friend, and
Staunch Defender of Good Sense

Contents

Prefatory Note

In the interests of readability the scholarly apparatus of these pages has been kept at a minimum. All quotations are identified by author or title in the course of the text, and full references to the sources appear under the author or the title in the "Works Cited" section at the end of the text. Bibliography for standard works such as Boswell's *Life of Johnson* and Wordsworth's *Prelude* is not given.

Introduction:

The Death

of Literature

If any young man could found a society where people speak only what they think and tell only what they know—in the first words that come to hand—that would be, at last, a school of literature.

But of course we must carry on. Prophets are no good: they get pupils and imitators and start silly fashions. God forgive us all! If I am accused on Judgment day of teaching literature, I shall plead that I never believed in it and that I maintained a wife and children. I don't know what old Bradley and G. Murray will plead, but I long to hear.

Sir Walter Raleigh, First Professor of English
Literature, Oxford University, Letter to George Gordon,
January 11, 1921

Literature has in the past thirty years or so passed through a time of radical disturbances that turned the institution and its primary values topsy-turvy. Talk began in the 1960s about the death of literature, with a comparison intended to Nietzsche's announcement of the death of God, and by 1982

Leslie Fiedler, a pop-lit advocate not sorry to see high-culture literature go, could happily title a book *What Was Literature?*

Internally, the traditional romantic and modernist literary values
have been completely reversed. The author, whose creative imagination
had been said to be the source of literature, was declared dead or the
mere assembler of various bits of language and culture into writings
that were no longer works of art but simply cultural collages or "texts."
The great historical tradition extending from Homer to the present has
been broken up in various ways. The influence of earlier poets on their
successors has been declared no longer beneficial but the source of
anxiety and weakness. The literary canon has been analyzed and
disintegrated, while literary history itself has been discarded as a
diachronic illusion, to be replaced by a synchronic paradigm. What
were once the masterpieces of literature, the plays of Shakespeare or
the novels of Flaubert, are now void of meaning, or, what comes to
the same thing, filled with an infinity of meanings, their language
indeterminate, contradictory, without foundation; their organizational
structures, grammar, logic, and rhetoric, verbal sleights of hand. Such
meaning as they may have is merely provisional and conferred on them
by the reader, not inherent in the text or set in place for all time by
the writer's word craft. Rather than being near-sacred myths of human
experience of the world and the self, the most prized possessions of
culture, universal statements about an unchanging and essential human nature, literature is increasingly treated as authoritarian and
destructive of human freedom, the ideology of the patriarchy devised
to instrument male, white hegemony over the female and the "lesser
breeds." Criticism, which was once the scorned servant of literature,
has declared its independence and insisted that it too is literature.
Not everyone accepts all of these new views, but their reality is increasingly taken as fact, and it is as fact, not a judgment of what has
happened, that they are here described in as neutral a way as possible.

Externally, political radicals, old and young, from Herbert Marcuse to Terry Eagleton, have attacked literature as elitist and repressive. Television and other forms of electronic communication have increasingly replaced the printed book, especially its idealized form, literature, as a more attractive and authoritative source of knowledge. Literacy, on which literary texts are dependent, has diminished to the point that we commonplacely speak of a "literacy crisis." Courses in composition have increasingly replaced courses in literature in the colleges and universities, where enrollments and majors in literature continue to decrease nationally. The art novel has grown increasingly involute and cryptic, poetry more opaque, gloomy, and inward, and theater more hysterical, crude, and vulgar in counterproductive attempts to assert their continued importance. What was once called "serious literature" has by now only a coterie audience, and almost no presence in the world outside university literature departments. Within the university, literary criticism, already by the 1960s Byzantine in its complexity, mountainous in its bulk, and incredible in its totality, has turned on literature and deconstructed its basic principles, declaring literature an illusory category, the poet dead, the work of art only a floating "text," language indeterminate and incapable of meaning, interpretation a matter of personal choice. Many of our best authors—Nabokov, Mailer, Malamud, and Bellow were the cases I explored in an earlier book, *The Imaginary Library*—have experienced and not recovered from a crisis of confidence in the traditional values of literature and a sense of its importance to humanity.

The disintegration of literature has become scandalous enough to produce headlines and bestsellers. In 1988, Stanford University, for example, made the front pages and the TV news programs with a debate about whether its required course in great books, including many works of literature, should drop some of the classics, all written by "dead white males," to make room for the inclusion of books by women, blacks, and Third World writers. The great books which had hitherto formed the basis of liberal education were denounced as elitist, Eurocentric, and the tools of imperialism. Under this kind of pressure, the faculty and administration agreed to replace such writers as Homer and Dickens with books like Simone de Beauvoir's *Second Sex*. William Bennett, then a conservative secretary of education, debated with the president of Stanford on national television the social question at the center of the issue: the relative importance to society at large of the traditional intellectual qualities represented by the classics of literature versus social values of equality of gender and race represented by less prestigious writings.

This particular debate was but one part of a wider cultural debate about the breakdown of education, and particularly literary education, raised in books that became surprise best-sellers, *Cultural Literacy* by E. Donald Hirsch, Jr., and *The Closing of the American Mind* by Allan Bloom. Hirsch, a professor of English literature at the University of Virginia, charging that Americans are becoming culturally illiterate from not reading the best kinds of writing, offered a test in great ideas—Darwin, Freud, Marx, for example—that could be administered at home to diagnose the seriousness of the deficiency. A follow-up volume provided in handy form the means to rectify the deficiency in case, like radon in the cellar, it should be discovered. Bloom, a University of Chicago professor of politics with a bias to literature, is a follower of Leo Strauss and his view of certain classic texts, Plato particularly, as the sacred repositories of arcane truths. He charged that a pliant relativism in university faculties, derived from Nietzsche and other German philosophers, had led education away from the classic texts and their Socratic search for the good and the true. The modern student, infected with relativism, believing that all values are only opinions, and one opinion as good as another, has entirely abandoned, according to Bloom, the great books and their quest for the best course of belief or action, to live in a daze of universal tolerance, apathy, and ignorance.

Even if Bennett, Hirsch, and Bloom are taken at something less than face value, the widespread interest in their views testifies to a general concern that book culture, of which literature is a central part, is disappearing, and with it many of our society's central values. No wonder Marxists fight feminists for the right to identify the smells arising from the literary corpse. Bad faith or phallocentrism? Hegemony or gynocide? It went so far that the religious leader of Iran, the infamous Ayatollah, could without fear of reprisal take out a contract on the life of the author of a novel found offensive to Islam. Within a month, or ere Salman Rushdie's books were old, Western publishers were holding an international book fair in Iran.

If *literature* has died, *literary activity* continues with unabated, if not increased, vigor, though it is increasingly confined to universities and colleges. Stories and poetry are written and read, plays are performed, and strenuous efforts made to write well. Publishers pay large advances for novels, literary prizes are given with increasing frequency and in larger amounts, and the literature printed, of whatever quality, continues to increase. An industrious literary criticism and scholarship, largely within the academies, overproduces both literary theory and practical criticism. There are many optimists who see a new and better literary system arising phoenixlike from the ashes of the old, no longer the "repository of known truth and received values" (Levine) but "a poetics which strives to define the conditions of meaning. . . . how we go about making sense of texts" (Culler). This redirection of literature is perceived by its supporters as a giant step for humankind, and Levine and his colleagues at a conference on the humanities spoke for the more advanced criticism when they said that it seems "particularly ironic that the humanities are receiving their most severe criticism at a moment when for many of us their significance and strength have never been greater."

What has passed, or is passing, is the romantic and modernist literature of Wordsworth and Goethe, Valéry and Joyce, that flourished in capitalistic society in the high age of print, between the mid-

eighteenth century and the mid-twentieth. The death of the old literature in the grand sense, Shelley's unacknowledged legislation of the
world, Arnold's timeless best that has been thought and written, Eliot's
unchanging monuments of the European mind, from the rock drawings
in Lascaux to *The Magic Mountain*, has seemed to people who matured
intellectually in the ancien régime of high culture nothing less than
the setting of the sun of the human imagination in the evening-lands
of Western civilization. No more eloquent defense of the old literary
order has appeared than a collection of essays, *Prose and Cons*, by
Maynard Mack, and no more bitter denunciation of the new ways than
one of the essays, "The Life of Learning": "We are narrowing, not
enlarging our horizons. We are shucking, not assuming our respon-
sibilities. And we communicate with fewer and fewer because it is
easier to jabber in a jargon than to explain a complicated matter in
the real language of men. How long can a democratic nation afford to
support a narcissistic minority so transfixed by its own image?" Many
others, like Mack, remember that it was only yesterday that F. R.
Leavis could reject C. P. Snow's argument in *The Two Cultures* that
humanists were dangerously ignorant of science with the haughty observation that a humane training based on literature was the only
education worth having. Cleanth Brooks and W. K. Wimsatt only a
few years ago claimed critical infallibility, as if their formalist conceptions of literature were revealed truth, anathematizing heterodoxy
as "the intentional fallacy" and "the heresy of paraphrase." Not long
ago at all, there seemed nothing absurd in Northrop Frye's argument
in *Anatomy of Criticism* that the totality of literature formed an extensive scheme, mystical in its symbolism, but orderly in its structure,
originating in the fears and desires constituting the human soul and
moving through history in the form of the great literary myths, cor-
responding with nothing less than the seasonal cycle of the natural
year.

Looking back, it seems incredible that these views could have so recently been taken as seriously as they surely were. But they are gone now, and to the often bewildered, muttering, and angry survivors of the old order, the change has seemed another treason of the clerks, who are most often identified as a group of radical critics practicing, usually in the universities, what Paul Ricoeur has aptly labeled "the hermeneutics of suspicion." Phenomenology, structuralism, deconstruction, Freudianism, Marxism, feminism have been the most clamorous voices announcing the death of the old literature in recent years. Structuralism and deconstruction, the leading demystifiers of traditional literary views for a time, were a poetics militant, attacking bourgeois society by undermining its ideology and exposing all authority, including all literary authority, as illegitimate and repressive. Feminism denounced the old literature as an instrument of male domination. Marxists, the followers of Foucault, and the new historicists treated literature as a capitalist institution and a disguised instrument of hegemony, to be exposed as mere establishment propaganda. To the new Freudians, literature was another form of the repression of instinct and revolutionary impulses, to be cured by deeper analysis.

The Anglo-Saxon tendency has been to keep literature and politics as widely separated as possible, but these recent types of radical criticism have, in the manner of the Continent and particularly of Paris, associated themselves, both in theory and in practice, with new-left politics and social theory. Literature has been seen as a soft area of bourgeois society, a place at which to get at and discredit capitalist ideology, to advance Third World, minority, and feminist causes, and to advocate permissiveness, openness, and freedom in all areas, sexual, interpretive, environmental.

But the social scene in which the hermeneutics of suspicion have flourished has been much larger than the narrow setting of universities, conferences of specialists, and salon politics of the literary subculture. They, and literature itself, have been only one small part of a much more extensive and deeper cultural change. Not only the arts but all our traditional institutions, the family and the law, religion and the state, have in recent years been coming apart in startling ways. The family is probably the most desperate battlefield in this massive social change: the pill, soaring divorce rates, custody battles, poor single-parent families headed by women, right-to-life and pro-choice struggles, two-career families, surrogacy, women's rights, battered wives and murdered families, the disappearance of traditional patterns of sexual differentiation, in vitro fertilization, casual attitudes toward sex, the appearance of new venereal diseases. There is good and bad in this catalog, as well as "purposes mistook / Fall'n on the inventors heads," but all are causing enormous stress in an old institution. The death throes of the nuclear family, along with the changes in other major social institutions, make the death of romantic literature seem but a trifle here. To see what has happened to literature as a part of the social revolution sometimes loosely styled postindustrialism that has been transforming modern life in the West, and to a lesser degree in the Second and Third worlds as well, provides both a historical setting in which to understand literary change and a scale which accurately measures its interesting but limited part in what has been going on. In the larger world, in fact, the death of literature may be chiefly interesting only for the precise schematic way in which it represents changes taking place elsewhere, as in the family, in more complicated and less obvious ways. The exact reversal of literary values, for example—poets are creative geniuses / the poet is dead, literary texts are supersaturated with meaning / literary texts are empty of meaning—offers almost a laboratory example of the revolutionary, as opposed to evolutionary, model of institutional change that Thomas Kuhn called "paradigm shift."

Poetry and literature have always preferred to take themselves more in metaphysical than in sociological terms—perhaps in an attempt to conceal their persistent social marginality. Literature has not, after all, played a very large part in the power games of our society, and is unlikely to do so in the future. Cosmic theories of art and literature come and go as readily as philosophies in *Candide*, but even when they are nominally materialistic, as in Taine's literary history turning on climate, or Marxist views of the cultural superstructure, they tend to avoid awareness of the ordinary conditions that are their social setting. But the history of literature has always been closely involved with such worldly things as royal courts, patronage, copyright laws, middle-class leisure, nationalism, democratic educational systems, steam-driven rotary presses, free markets, and linotype machines.

The scene of writing and reading in recent times has been no less broadly social, and the disintegration of romantic-modernist literature in the late twentieth century has been a part not only of a general cultural revolution but more specifically of a technological revolution that is rapidly transforming a print to an electronic culture. In ways I have analyzed in an earlier book, *Samuel Johnson and the Impact of Print*, the old literature of romanticism and modernism was a printed-book concept from the outset, institutionalizing and idealizing print's potential to create authors, fix exact texts, hold the smallest detail of style locked permanently in place for leisured inspection, and assemble and catalog the imaginary library of universal literature. Literature began to lose its authority, and consequently its reality, at the same time that the ability to read the book, literacy, was decreasing, that audiovisual images, film, television, and computer screen, were replacing the printed book as the most efficient and preferred source of entertainment and knowledge. Television, computer database, Xerox, word processor, tape, and VCR are not symbiotic with literature and its values in the way that print was, and new ways of acquiring, storing, and transmitting information are signaling the end of a conception of writing and reading oriented to the printed book and institutionalized as literature. Each time that literature appears in one of these new contexts it encounters the world and feels its pressures on ways of thinking and doing.

Cultural obsolescence, at least as much as *Götterdämmerung*, has overtaken the old literature in a world where television is transforming everything it touches—politics, news, religion—where increasing numbers of citizens have great difficulty reading even simple texts, where creativity and plagiarism are increasingly hard to define, where advertising and image making have captured the language. The pressure of these new ways of doing things and thinking about things is felt at the many points where literature and its poetics interact in day-to-day activity with the social world: copyright cases, political patronage in the arts, books printed on acid paper disintegrating in libraries, distinguished professors and trendy clerics trying to define literature in a courtroom hearing a pornography case, schoolrooms where children who watch television eight hours a day can't read, decisions about who defines the words included in dictionaries, faculty fights about the establishment of new categories of study and departments, tax laws on publishers' inventories, charges of plagiarism, murderers writing about their crimes.

These and other places where the old literature is ceasing to be plausible or useful under the pressures of new circumstances in the late twentieth century are the settings of the following chapters. In them recent events in literature look startlingly different than they do in the light of the lamp. Deconstructive criticism, for example, which looms so large in the literary scene alone, figuring either as heroic revolutionary or treasonous clerk, when seen in the social context of the literacy crisis, or of the battle to control the language, begins to look far less melodramatic and more like criticism at its traditional social function of preserving whatever can be saved in a time of radical questioning of basic institutional values and beliefs. The death of literature looks like the twilight of the gods to conservatives or the fall of the Bastille of high culture to radicals, but my argument is, to put it simply, that we are watching the complex transformations of a social institution in a time of radical political, technological, and social change.

1

Ideology as Aesthetics:

The Politics of Romantic

and Modern Literature

In the Renaissance and the Enlightenment, the courts and
the aristocracy fostered the arts, and poetry was defined in
ways that suited ruling-class interests and values. Most of
the writers were men, rarely women, of taste and means, or,
like William Shakespeare, Gent., who bought a coat of arms,
they pretended to gentility and made every effort to acquire
property. The crown controlled all writing, directly through
censorship and patronage, and indirectly through a courtly
poetics that eventually developed into the firmnesses of neo-
classicism. Imitation of the ancients, maintenance of deco-
rum, and the observance of such rules as the unities in order
to control the sprawl of native writing gave aesthetic form to
such aristocratic social values as hierarchy, restraint, and
rigidly codified behavior.

Courtly poetry decayed rapidly during the course of the
eighteenth century, when the historical shifts we collectivize
as the French Revolution and the Industrial Revolution were
making aristocratic and authoritarian kingdoms into liberal
parliamentary societies, agricultural into capitalist econo-
mies. Science was at the same time replacing religion as the

11

primary epistemology, and an orientation toward tradition and the past was swinging toward the future and progress. Among these momentous changes, Western Europe was also transformed conclusively, three centuries after the appearance of the printing press, from an oral to a print culture. Mechanical and democratic print brought the pressures for change being exerted everywhere directly to bear on the old court-centered aristocratic poetry and belles lettres that had lasted from Dante and Petrarch to the days of Swift and Pope. Print created an open marketplace for books and ideas, made censorship and patronage uneconomic, transferred literary power to an increasingly literate public of "common readers," as Samuel Johnson styled them, and fostered a new type of professional writers who made their livings and reputations by providing what the market would buy. Samuel Johnson in England, Jean-Jacques Rousseau in France, and Gothold Lessing in Germany represented in their different ways these new professional writers of the print era, which for the first time included women, Hester Lynch Piozzi, Anna Letitia Barbauld, Hannah More, Frances Burney, Elizabeth Inchbald, and Maria Edgworth, to name only the most notable in England.

Johnson's famous letter to Lord Chesterfield—asserting that the author, not the aristocratic patron, owned the King's English that Johnson had just made the author's English in a dictionary defining words by the usage of the best writers—formally marks the end of the old courtly order of polite letters. It was also the beginning of what would in the romantic future become literature when authors like Wordsworth, Coleridge, and Goethe, and men of letters like Herder, Hazlitt, Sainte-Beuve, and Arnold established a different way of thinking about literary things.

The term *literature* began to be used in its modern sense only in the later eighteenth century. It was then that it began to shed its earlier meanings of "all serious writing" or of "anything written," or even "the ability to read," and to replace the slightly older "polite letters" and the much older "poetry" as a general term for what was now considered the best *imaginative* writing, regardless of genre—lyric, epic, dramatic—prose as well as verse. The philosopher and historian David Hume's intention, expressed in his autobiography, printed in 1777, the year after his death, "to regard every object as contemptible, except the improvement of my talents in literature," uses the word in its older sense, though with something of the newer romantic intensity. Judging from the context, Wordsworth pretty clearly intends the newer modern sense when he argues in 1800 in the preface to the second edition of *Lyrical Ballads* that science, not prose, is the true opposite of poetry, and speaks of "revolutions not of literature alone, but likewise of society."

The shift from courtly poetry in its neoclassical form to romantic literature was only one part of a larger rearranging of the categories of art that was taking place in the later eighteenth century. At the same time that poetry was becoming literature, it was also becoming one of the "arts," a category that was replacing such earlier cultural bundlings as the liberal arts, or, earlier still, the nine muses. Poetry, music, painting, sculpture, and dance were finally brought together in the mid-1700s as the fine arts, distinguished from mere skill or the craft of artisans by dropping any workaday function, such as providing information or moral instruction, and making pleasure achieved through beauty their sole function. Paul Oscar Kristeller describes the general social process by which various crafts became "art," and poetry was transformed into literature:

> The various arts are certainly as old as human civilization, but the manner in which we are accustomed to group them and to assign them a place in our scheme of life and of culture is comparatively recent. This fact is not as strange as may appear on the surface. In the course of history, the various arts change not only their content and style, but also their relations to each other, and their place in the general system of culture, as do

religion, philosophy or science. Our familiar system of the five fine arts did not merely originate in the eighteenth century, but it also reflects particular cultural and social conditions of that time.

The modern conception of the beaux arts, including first poetry, then literature, was established and spread by Diderot's *Encyclopédie*. Philosophical and psychological foundations for the arts were supplied by Kant, in whose *Critique of Judgment* beauty became along with truth and goodness an a priori category of human thought, thus making literature and the other arts, in their expression of the sublime and the beautiful, equal in importance with the metaphysics that expressed truth and the ethics that objectified goodness.

Never as central as religion, the family, the law, or the state—the four great institutional pillars of society—art nonetheless became an important part of the furnishings of modern Western culture. In T. S. Eliot's famous phrasing in "Tradition and the Individual Talent," the "existing monuments" of art form "an ideal order among themselves," embodying the mind and the conscience of Europe. In literature that "ideal order" was objectified during the nineteenth century in a canon of writings composed of all works created by the imagination, prose as well as poetry, and all genres, the novel as well as the epic, of all places and times—including Chinese court tales, Indian religious books, primitive epics, Christian hymns, Persian idylls, folk ballads, and exquisite court verse forms. In practice the Western works took precedence, and Western poetics were always dominant; but in theory at least literature was a universal product of the human imagination. Scholars constructed a continuous literary history, beginning with oral poetry among the Greeks, and established a secure place for literature in the great historical eras as, for example, the expression of Athenian democracy, Enlightenment rationalism, or fin de siècle aestheticism. The great characters of literature—Oedipus, Aeneas, Falstaff, Don

Quixote, Tartuffe, Faust, Pip, Emma Bovary, Stephen Dedalus—became the most real of people. The authors' lives—Horace on his Sabine farm, Petrarch climbing Mount Ventoux, Samuel Johnson kicking the stone at Harwich, Jane Austen writing in her room while visiting relations in the country, Joyce and Nora in Trieste—added further substance to literature's reality.

Literature was from the beginning a text-centered institution, and the masterpieces of literary art, *The Iliad, Hamlet, War and Peace, Remembrance of Things Past,* each with its meaning structured firmly in its form, were its central reality. To speak of "literature" is still to mean the printed books that stand rank on bibliographic rank in the world's libraries, where "literature" has become a standard category of knowledge, ordered and reified in the cataloging system. What was only a concept for the great romantics solidified during the nineteenth and twentieth centuries into a social institution of considerable dimensions and firmness. The collections of the great national research libraries built up in the nineteenth century objectified literature, while its increasing appearance in the schools and in the university curriculum testified to its importance as a mode of knowledge. The scholarly and critical activities that grew up around teaching literature thickened its existential weave with an extensive secondary literature of literary history and theory, poetics, concordances, anthologies, textual studies, biographies, and bibliographies.

Appearing in conjunction with an intellectual, political, and economic revolution, literature was originally allied—"Bliss was it in that dawn to be alive"—with forces that overthrew kings and swept away impediments to freedom. A list of names like Shelley, Heine, Hugo, Lorca, Brecht, Sartre, and Mailer testifies that literature never entirely abandoned its early revolutionary zeal, even though individual writers like Goethe, Wordsworth, Yeats, and T. S. Eliot adjusted, compromised, or went into reaction. But as the features of the bourgeois state began to emerge from enlightenment and revolution, and 1789 gave way to 1830 and 1848, literature and the other arts, still identifying with the original idealism of revolution, chose increasingly to be at odds with the new world of money, cities, factories, and machines portrayed most extensively in France by Balzac and in England by Dickens.

The emerging critical attitude appears in concentrated form in the literary typology of the bourgeois towns and cities, Flaubert's soul-destroying Yonville, Thompson's city of dreadful night, Blake's dark Satanic London, Balzac's Paris, Dickens's Coketown, Eliot's dead polyglot metropolis, "unreal city." In a few places—Dreiser's Chicago, or Baudelaire's *Paris le fourmillant tableau*—the modern city fascinates with its power and shines with the evil rising from its decay, but the standard literary view has been Flaubert's contemptuous remark in a letter to Louise Colet in 1852, "What can you expect from a population which, like Manchester's, spends its life making pins?" Or Ruskin's outrage: "The great cry that rises from all our manufacturing cities, louder than their furnace blast, is all in very deed for this—that we manufacture everything there except men; we blanch cotton, and strengthen steel, and refine sugar, and shape pottery; but to brighten, to strengthen, to refine or to form a single living spirit, never enters into our estimate of advantage."

Wordsworth's *Prelude, or Growth of a Poet's Mind*, written first in the 1790s and corrected constantly until its publication after his death in 1850, charts the course that literature would take in the nineteenth century. At a time when the population across Europe was leaving the land for the cities and work in its factories, to build and pay for progress, the poet in the opening of *The Prelude*, as he had earlier rejected the terror and imperialism of the French Revolution, turns away from London, the "monstrous anthill of the plain," and plunges deep into nature and the rural past of a small village and isolated house among the lakes and mountains of Westmoreland. At a time when scientific rationalism was becoming the dominant mode of official thought, reducing life to calculation and cold logic, the poet, choosing himself as hero and his poetic vocation as his subject, rejecting his formal Cambridge education, plunges deep into himself. There he seeks to recover in his memories, even as he had in nature, the memories of the vivid sensations of childhood, which provide in the depressed and limited states of adulthood the famous "intimations of immortality." His artistic imagination is renewed by finding in these stored experiences a lost sense of authentic being and a deeply felt and secure religious meaning to life and in nature. The world is good, the poet discovers, and its goodness, though only intermittently felt, is to be found in the past, the primitive, the irrational, in nature, in childhood, and in the flood of imaginative joy that comes in those moments of intense revelation that Wordsworth called "spots of time" and Joyce would call "epiphanies." In the end, poetry is justified as the voice of mighty powers, now obscured by modern civilization, and the poet and his imagination, chosen by some unseen power for the noble task, are their vessel and prophet.

The Prelude set the program for romanticism—nature, the primitive, deep consciousness, the irrational, art—and to only a somewhat lesser extent for modernism. Generations of authors have lived out the poet's role that Wordsworth created, in life and poem, withdrawing from industrialized society and rejecting its materialistic values. Sometimes they took up their stance on the left, like Blake and Shelley, sometimes on the right like Yeats and Pound, but always, like Joyce's Stephen Dedalus, they refused to bow—non serviam—to the bourgeois family, religion, nation, and language that they felt cast nets over their souls. The romantic artist—Byron the exile, Flaubert the dedicated and lonely high priest of the word, Strindberg the mad misogynist, or Oscar Wilde mocking the marquis of Queensbury in his trial for sodomy—has been the man from underground, the alienated one, his own hero and his own subject, proudly, defiantly different from the middle-class businessmen he scorned. In the words of Flaubert, advising Louise

Colet in 1853 how she must live if she is to be the true artist, "Art, like the Jewish God, wallows in sacrifices. So tear yourself to pieces, mortify your flesh, roll in ashes, smear yourself with filth and spittle, wrench out your heart! You will be alone, your feet will bleed, an infernal disgust will be with you throughout your pilgrimage, what gives joy to others will give none to you, what to them are but pinpricks will cut you to the quick, and you will be lost in the hurricane with only beauty's faint glow visible on the horizon."

"Sappho" took Flaubert's advice with a grain of salt, but the role has remained valid, even in the modern period of art and literature since the Great War. Though many of the other flamboyances of romanticism were abandoned by modernism, the artist has suffered from a distinct cultural lag, remaining as truculent as Hemingway or Mailer, as tormented as Lowell or Plath, as defiantly perverse as Tennessee Williams or Andrea Dworkin. The skeleton of the Flaubertian artist remains visible in William S. Burroughs, the son of a rich industrialist, who has taken the role of the *poète maudit* just about as far as it can go:

> Traumatized by an incident of sexual abuse in his childhood that he has never quite been able to recall, he becomes a social pariah, drops into the underworld, takes up drugs, explores homosexuality, rolls drunks in New York City subways, flees the police from Texas to Mexico City to Tangiers to London to Paris. The horror of killing his wife [while shooting a glass of gin off her head] dissolves his writer's block. In 'Junky,' 'Naked Lunch' and the trilogy comprising 'The Soft Machine,' 'The Ticket that Exploded' and 'Nova Express,' he smashes linear narrative and explores the last frontiers of forbidden subject matter.

This description of Burroughs must have been written tongue in cheek, though the cultural pages of the *New York Times* are the Camelot of the last romantics, but Christopher Lehmann-Haupt's words show that

Orwell was clearly either behind or ahead of his time when he remarked of Ezra Pound that "one has the right to expect ordinary decency even of a poet."

Scientific rationalism has been the official mode of knowledge in modern society, but the artist has inevitably been distinguished by possession of its mirror opposite, an intuitive power to create art and literature out of the creative imagination, a gnostic psychic faculty conceived of as a divine energy in the depths of the authentic self, bringing meaning into the world. The definitions of the imagination have ranged from Coleridge's godlike "repetition in the finite mind of the eternal act of creation in the infinite I AM," to the symbolists' and surrealists' creator of images of supernatural luminosity, Yeats's visions and automatic writing, Freud's primary language of the unconscious and dream work, Jung's symbols of the collective unconscious, Richards's balancing of appetencies, and dream states, ouija boards and drug induced visions, opium once, now LSD and cocaine. Moderate critics may call the psychic energy that generates literature and art no more than "emotion" or "sensitivity" and tie it closely to the daylight faculties, but more radical critics distinguish primary and secondary imaginations, and speak of "visionary power," the "primal unconscious" and even "race memory." But whatever the poetry-making power has been called, romanticism has constantly made it the essential energy of creative literature, making lovelier and truer things than the rational mind can discover in its laboratories and with its computers, whose bits are only "sands upon the Red Sea shore / Where Israel's tents do shine so bright."

Behind the images of the imaginative and creative artist, in life like James Joyce, in art like Stephen Dedalus, nineteenth- and twentieth-century writers and critics gradually built up a supporting poetics that defined the literary work of art in ways that precisely opposed it to bourgeois materialism and its consumer products. The chief instrument and primary symbol of industrialism has been the machine, and literature itself was a cultural development of a machine, the printing press. But literature, forgetful always of its technological foundations, has consistently identified with the anti-mechanical, with nature and the natural, with the organic, the intrinsic, the spontaneous, the magical and mysterious, the human and the humane. Symbolism and aestheticism made literary style shine with an aura of Platonic brightness that condemned the crude, styleless products of industrial society as ugly, shapeless factory junk. The machine without pause or variation turns out an endless stream of mass-produced identical commodities for sale in the marketplace, so art became the expression of unpredictable and surprising creative genius, the unique work of the creative individual. Adam Smith's market, utilitarian and pragmatic, sets the value of commodities at the price they can command by their availability or functionality, but the literary artwork was distinguished by its practical uselessness, its "pricelessness," its total removal from any dollars-and-cents considerations.

When in the course of time, the technology of industrial society produced its own artistic media and its own arts, the phonograph and tape recording, photography and the motion picture, television and the VCR, the poster and reprints of masterpieces, electronic music, the cheap mass-produced comic book or paperback fiction—western, romance, whodunit, and sci-fi—high culture long rejected this mass or pop art as vulgar and spurious because it was made in large numbers by the machine to suit democratic tastes. Walter Benjamin's famous essay, "The Work of Art in the Age of Mechanical Reproduction," gave classic statement to the reasoning that supported this continued rejection of the products of the machine. Machines that produce popular art—the printing press, camera, and sound recorder are Benjamin's examples—vitiate what they make by producing endless exact copies, duplicates, that strip the original artwork—picture, statue, theatrical performance, or the publicly told oral tale—of its "aura." This "aura" in Benjamin's sense is the special cultic potency the art work possessed by virtue of its uniqueness and its specific and individual historical provenance. It is an odd argument for a Marxist, since it attacks the popular art of the proletariat, who are amused even while being exploited by it, while making the defining quality of great art an "aura" that can only surround its objects in the courts of kings, the art galleries of the nobility, and the collections of the plutocrats, where they, the only instances of what they are, stand alone and isolated from the rest of the world. But Marxism is at root a romantic ideology, appearing in the high age of romanticism, and Benjamin was always most attracted to that aspect of historical materialism.

Eventually a number of the lively arts made by the machine and industrial technology were accepted as true art. Film—both photography and cinema—and some popular music—certainly jazz, a few musicals, folk songs, and perhaps some rock. But they became art not in the terms of their technological and social origins—mass produced, standard value, consumer products—but by being endowed with the qualities of individual creativity and style that defined high art. Romantic art has never forgiven industrial society to the point of admitting that it has been able to further the traditional arts and even create new energetic arts of its own, but rather has made these popular arts over in the image of high art, turning them against the social order and the technology that generated them. The film is now more virulent in its criticism of all forms of authority, political, sexual, or intellectual, than were the romantic poets, and the electronically played and amplified music and lyrics of rock are so radically subversive that politicians can win votes, and media coverage, by campaigning against them.

No longer imitative or didactic but imaginatively creative—a lamp illuminating the darkness of the unknown rather than a mirror reflecting the given world, to use the images Meyer Abrams made famous— literature claimed to express the true human spirit speaking through the imagination for beauty, for sweetness and light, or for a disinterested art for art's sake. Privileged by its beauty, form, style, craft, structure, the perfected art object—Keats's Grecian urn, the "unravished bride of quietness," Yeats's artificial bird of "hammered gold and gold enameling"—has stood in absolute opposition to the ugliness of industrialism, the crudeness of its products, the utilitarianism of its values, the philistinism of its attitudes, and the vulgarity of a life defined by the cash nexus.

Aesthetics, a term coined expressly to designate romantic art values, has stressed the formal properties of art, above all, style. Style achieved in every aspect of the work, sound patterns, syntax, imagery and tropes, characters, and plots culminating in the wholeness, harmony and radiance, in Joyce's terms in *Portrait of the Artist*, of the perfected work of art. Flaubert's desire, in a famous letter of 1852, to be done with mimesis and the subservience of the writer to the world, catches perfectly the essentialism of style in literature. He wanted to write, he said, "a book about nothing, a book dependent on nothing external, which would be held together by the strength of its style." Craft and style were most often grounded in psychology, being said to be the natural language of the poetic imagination, but they were so central to literature that they tended to acquire a life of their own. Style is "one of those names," said Valéry, "whose musical quality suggests a language whose words sound out their meaning."

If the literary work was style, its stories were myths. Not for literature the drab and emotionally empty facts of science, but modern versions of the rituals and tales collected in Sir James Fraser's *Golden Bough*, which, though written to show the triumph of science over magic, became for the literary world a treasure trove of myths and a validation of their centrality in human life. To treat literature as myth, rather than mere story or narrative, had many advantages. It connected literature in another way with the ancient past of the race, always a desideratum, and it freed literature from merely reproducing pictures of a debased here and now. Above all, however, in a rationalistic society rigidly shunning superstition and the irrational, literature as myth set itself up as a competing and superior way of knowing to science. Not just storytelling or make-believe, literature as myth offered modern versions of ancient myths of origin, of the numinous and the taboo, reworkings of antique rites of scapegoat and initiation, inspired remembrances of the hero with a thousand faces and the journey through the sterile lands of the Fisher King.

Not all literature was so explicitly mythical as Blake's visionary cycles, or Browning's *Childe Roland to the Dark Tower Came*, or Joyce's *Ulysses* and *Finnegans Wake*, but by speaking of its stories as myth in a loose and general way, literature gave itself an aura of mystery and asserted that it retold the primary stories about what has always been feared and desired in all places and times. It also found a potent imagery in those persistent cultural symbols, the circle of perfection, the cross of suffering, the sun of reason and the moon of imagination, the opposition of chaos and order, the lamb and the tiger, which it made into an iconography of literature.

In its most secular form, literature's portrayal of itself as myth claimed no access to the mysteries of the ancient past, but only a modern power to do now what myth has always done, to make up stories that give the world meaning in a satisfactorily human way. By providing new heroes, like the detective and the spy, and new stories, like science fiction and the western, and new symbols, like the computer Hal with a will of its own in the film *2001*, literature, usually of the popular variety, is said to be mythic in its ability to focus and interpret the fragmented experiences of modern life, giving meaning and thereby purpose to people for whom science and a rationalized religion no longer provide life-sustaining explanations.

Imagination, creativity, style, myth—these have been the key terms of literature. No one ever assembled them in a complete and authoritative poetics, organizing the dispersed and fragmentary occasional criticism into some grand literary summa. There have been a few distinguished megacritical attempts of very different kinds, for example, Shelley's *Defence of Poetry*, Arnold's *Culture and Anarchy*, the Chadwicks' *Growth of Literature*, Wellek's and Warren's *Theory of Literature*, and Frye's *Anatomy of Criticism*, but the poetics of literature have remained, with results we will consider in the next chapter, more a series of ad hoc essays and remarks than a systematic poetics.

Literature has always presented itself as autonomous and independent of the society it has existed to attack. Literary metaphysics were offered as transcendent truths, emerging spontaneously from the realms of the sublime, of beauty and form, out of the inner depths of the self, the primitive and authentic energies of imaginative being, reappearing mysteriously from the submerged and mysterious past. But, as we have just seen, the primary values of literature were always mirror opposites of the dominant realities of a society of money, machines, parliaments, factories, cities, and laboratories. For all its fierce hostility to the bourgeoisie and the world they made, literature has always been a part, if only a negative part, of the social system it rejected. It also has been de facto, for better or for worse, *the* literary system of modern Western capitalist society, with an officially recognized function of fostering creativity and expressing the higher aspirations of the human spirit. The modern world, of course, has never assigned to art, and especially to literature, a central place in the scheme of things, but it has given creative artists and their work a place of at least some dignity, accepting literature as a subject of instruction in the educational system, giving it a legal reality in courts that protected it with copyright and exempted it from the slander standards imposed on other types of discourse.

Only the societies of the modern Western world have been wealthy, confident, and tolerant enough to support institutions like literature whose raison d'être has been to criticize the established social order and its central values. In more traditional societies, all institutions function strictly as legitimators of the existing order, and even in modern Western society other institutions, like religion, the media, and the law, that to some degree criticize the establishment, always end as the stoutest defenders of the status quo, revealing weakness only to preserve strength. University subjects such as history and economics also regularly understand their interests as closely linked with those of the world. Only the arts, and particularly literature, continue at every opportunity to bite the hand that feeds them.

Marxists, with their view of cultural superstructure determined by industrial and ideological infrastructure, have always insisted that despite appearances to the contrary, there has been from the beginning a close connection between romantic art and the capitalist state. Marx and Engels spoke in *The Communist Manifesto* of the intellectual assemblage of a universal literature in the early nineteenth century as a characteristic capitalist expropriation of the resources of undeveloped countries: "From the numerous national and local literatures, there [arose] a world literature." In this view, universal literature was assembled in the same way and for the same reasons that imperialism plundered the world in the age of primitive accumulation to create a worldwide marketplace in which to sell its goods. For Marxist critics, the literature of the nineteenth and twentieth centuries, under the mask of apparent criticism of capitalist society, in fact provided apologies for the imperialism, racism, male hegemony, and other forms of oppression that are supposed to be characteristic of capitalism. Art has been seen as "commodity fetishism" and "the opiate of the intellectuals," a way of harmlessly bleeding off antisocial pressures, the anarchic elements that mess up complex societies, the discontents that Freud saw as inescapable in civilizations that restrain libido as severely as capitalistic society.

Marxist criticism need not be accepted at full face value to recognize the correctness of its underlying argument that despite the revolutionary mythology of romanticism there is and always has been a close working connection between literature and its parent society.

When we begin looking in the direction the Marxists point we can see, for example, that the role of the artist, while a bit raffish, still idealizes the primary middle-class values of individualism and creativity, and that the perfect work of art owned in perpetuity and in a special, almost sacred, sense by its creator is an idealization of Lockean property rights based on labor. Literature emphasizes the new and the novel, originality and uniqueness being primary characteristics of true artists and true art, even as the industrial world seeks and rewards progress through constant improvement and change. Creativity and inventiveness are highly prized both in the arts and in business, and skillful making and intricate structuring, while they may mean different things in different workplaces, are as familiar to engineers as to poets. Art and literature give all these values a distinct twist, but it takes no particular ingenuity to see that art and capitalism meet and reinforce one another in such shared values as property, work, creativity, individualism, and change.

Shaw was the poet of this normally concealed relationship of modern industry and art. Against a background of conventional beliefs about the absolute difference between the poet and the businessman, he delighted in showing the close connection of the two through the paradox of the muddled men-of-the-world and the clearheaded poet, Marchbanks in *Candida* or Dubedat in *The Doctors' Dilemma*. Or, reversing the mechanism, he gave us poetic politicians like Caesar and Napoleon, or imaginative businessmen like Undershaft, who run circles around orthodox artists and intellectuals. Shaw showed imagination and clear thinking as the forces that drive the world along, and on his stage, as in the world, they are to be found in the professions and in business as well as in the arts. No wonder Yeats, like other romantics, disliked him so much, comparing him to a great sewing machine, smiling and smiling with his big white teeth while turning out endless cynical paradoxes.

But in spite of the growing obviousness of the relationship, literature and the other arts have relentlessly continued to reject any identification with the modern world. The passionate words of the artist-designer William Morris describe the present-day views of the professors of literature and the avant-garde writers of 1990 as accurately as they did the bright-eyed romantics of an earlier era:

> Apart from the desire to produce beautiful things, the leading passion of my life has been and is hatred of modern civilization. . . . What shall I say concerning its mastery of and its waste of mechanical power, its commonwealth so poor, its enemies of the commonwealth so rich, its stupendous organization— for the misery of life! Its contempt of simple pleasures, which everyone could enjoy but for its folly? Its cycless vulgarity which has destroyed art. . . . The struggles of mankind for many ages have produced nothing but this sordid, aimless, ugly confusion.

Literary people at all levels continue to believe and act out this same bitter hostility toward the main line of modern society, as if criticism of the social order, of politicians and businessmen, were the sine qua non of the arts. Failure to acknowledge and act on the actual situation of the arts in modern society, even as they become obvious to everyone, continues to condemn them to a place of mockery and irrelevance in the social world, the only world in which they can and do exist. It also commits the arts still to the romantic ideology—the creative imagination of the artist, the unique and perfect work of art, the magic of style and the mystery of myth—that was developed in direct opposition to capitalist society.

But as that society itself has changed from Coketown and its dark satanic mills, so the romantic ideology has come to seem increasingly implausible toward the end of the twentieth century. It still has its true believers, of course, and there are many, particularly in the "fine" arts, who continue literally to believe in artists as special people and art as sacred. And the law is, as we shall see, busily engaged in adapting hardline romantic aesthetics to the ends of modern greed and the cult of personality. But by and large, in the changed social and technological contexts we will be looking at shortly, these romantic ideas have lost their vigor and their ability to persuade. Inside the literary world they have been totally discredited by a generation of deconstructive critics, while outside, in both literature and the arts, they have become a kind of public joke. The cultural flavor of the situation and its inconsequentiality were caught exactly in a recent replay of the old art farce of outraging the citizenry and opposing the magistrates.

By 1989 everyone knew their parts perfectly. The artists came on first. In Chicago a gallery arranged an exhibit in such a way as to require stepping on the American flag. In Washington a planned showing of Robert Mapplethorpe's sadomasochistic photographs included pictures of a black man pissing in a white man's mouth and men trussed up in various ingenious contrivances of chain, pulleys, and leather. As was pointed out at the time, the newspapers, magazines, and TV programs that were the staunchest defenders of the freedom of art could not and did not try to show Mapplethorpe's actual pictures. The Mapplethorpe exhibition had been assembled, using federal funds, by the Institute for Contemporary Art at the University of Pennsylvania. In North Carolina a more than usually desperate and avant member of the art garde, Andres Serrano, who had been supported by the Southeastern Center for Contemporary Art, in Winston-Salem, with National Endowment money, displayed a photograph of a crucifix immersed in his urine. A hot summer, a surplus of urine, a lot of old-fashioned romantic and modernist posing, and a very up-to-date thirst for media exposure!

The politicians knew their parts as well as did the artists. The Supreme Court had recently ruled that the First Amendment guaranteed the right to burn the flag, or, by extension, to defile it in any way that seemed interesting, attractive, and necessary to free expression. The president proposed an amendment to the Constitution to prohibit any irreverent treatment of the flag. But Congress merely passed a law forbidding mistreatment of the flag, which two Princeton students immediately defied by burning a flag on Cannon Green to demonstrate that they would endure no restraints on individual freedom. Congress thundered that it would cut off the funding for the arts because public money had sponsored the putative works of art that outraged the common decency of the taxpayers. Senator Alfonse D'Amato, Republican of New York, tore a catalog showing the Serrano crucifix in urine to shreds on the floor of the Senate and proceeded to stomp on it. Jesse Helms, Republican senator from North Carolina, introduced an amendment to the funding bill for the National Endowment for the Arts (*New York Times, July 27, 1989*) that barred the use of federal funds to "promote, disseminate or produce obscene or indecent materials, including but not limited to depictions of sadomasochism, homoeroticism, the exploitation of children, or individuals engaged in sex acts; or material which denigrates the objects or beliefs of the adherents of a particular religion or nonreligion." It is that "or nonreligion" that gives the special senatorial firk to the language, but however ludicrous, the result was a cut in the appropriation and a denial of federal money to the agencies that sponsored the Mapplethorpe and Serrano works for a five-year period.

Then it was the turn of the experts. The general position was the familiar one that the government had no business censoring art or trying to define its subject. "Art often deals with the extremities of the human condition. It is not to be expected that when it does that, everyone is going to be pleased or happy with it," one museum director smoothly remarked. Robert Brustein, an actor-director with many a past triumph in shocking audiences in the Yale and Harvard theaters, assaulted the government for *not having given enough to the arts*, as if somehow more money would have prevented, or at least made more acceptable, what he called "flout[ing] prevailing codes." He went on to complain that "federal subsidy of the arts in our country accounts for only about 5 percent of the total budgets of established arts institutions, as compared to between 60 and 100 percent in more civilized nations." West Germany turned out to be the most civilized in this respect, as it so often has in the past, giving "$6 *billion* to theater alone." Brustein ended with the familiar old warnings about imposing "punitive moral constraints on independent esthetic activity" and reminded the politicians that "it is on the basis of quality, not morality, that posterity judges art." The proposed reduction of funding for the arts brought even more anguished howls of protest, "Federal interference with the freedom of the arts"; "every cultural institution in the country should be chilled by this"; we are "being punished for doing exactly what we are supposed to do: challenge the public to see, think and discuss critical issues of our culture and society." In the end everyone connected with the arts expressed outrage at what they considered the right of art to define its own subject. The Corcoran Gallery apologized to its curators and to America's artists for its temerity in canceling the display of Mapplethorpe's photographs on the grounds that they might offend public taste and risk the gallery's federal funding. All was in vain, and eventually the board put the director under heavy pressure and despite abject apologies many artists said that they would not exhibit at the Corcoran in the future. Shortly afterward, when the Helm amendment had become law, the director of the National Endowment for the Arts nearly had his head torn off by the New York art establishment—Leonard Bernstein refused to allow the president of the United States to give him a cultural award—when he revoked a ten-thousand-dollar grant to an exhibit for those with AIDS that had criticized Senator Helms and several other politicians in its catalog. The heat was too high, and in the end the director crumbled and, trying to save face, restored the grant to the exhibit, though not to the offensive catalog.

There is no real intellectual life in all this, only the acting out of traditional romantic art-attitudes in the interests of politics, prestige, money, and social power, which are no longer in accordance with understood realities, such as the fact that that art is only what its parent society says it is. For all the fury that the art world mustered in the defense of the power itself to define art, and to claim all the attendant publicity, to the world at large the Mapplethorpe-Helm affair is only further proof that the arts are the province of the loony left with no real bearing on the serious matters of the world, and to those who think about such matters it is simply a tired repetition of conventional views that assume that art is a particular and definite kind of object, that its chief end is epatering the bourgeois, and that it is of such critical importance to the world that it should be supported by the society it mocks. These are, for all the energy with which they are acted out, the attitudes more suitable to another time and place than late twentieth-century America, and if literature and the other arts are to play some meaningful part in social life in years to come, their relationship to the established order needs to be thought through again and redefined. Art is, after all, not some definite object like shovels, nor some given reality like mountains, it is whatever a society says is art at any given time, and it does what people agree that art should do. It can be a bad joke, as it is in the Mapplethorpe-Serrano-Helms business, where the received concept of art is badly out of place in present-day society, or it can be a concept and an activity that serve human needs and enlist the honest respect of the society in which it must exist.

2

Lady Chatterley and

"Mere Chatter about Shelley":

The University Asked

to Define Literature

If at an earlier time literature existed primarily in the royal court and its extensions, the church and the great house, and after that in the booksellers' shops and the homes of middle-class educated readers, its residence now is largely an academic setting, in the universities and their departments of literature. There still is, of course, a writing and publishing world outside the academy, usually stiffly superior to and scornful of professors, in the manner of Gore Vidal, for example, but literature has been almost entirely institutionalized by now inside the university.

The older literature—anything, say, written much more than a generation ago—is talked about and read only in the university classrooms and libraries. But it is not only the older works, Chaucer, Shakespeare, Milton, that are preserved by teaching and kept in print by classroom demand for texts. The literature of the present increasingly has its life inside the academic walls as well. Creative writing has become a major subject of instruction, poets and novelists are supported as writers in residence, and university presses are becoming publishers of poetry and of the art novel as well as almost the sole publisher of literary history and criticism. It is almost exclusively in the university that any theoretical discussion of literary matters takes place, and there too that the literary texts are edited, biographies of the older authors written, concordances assembled, literary history constructed, and a host of other practical activities performed that help to keep the institution of literature actual and meaningful in the world.

Minor exceptions can be made to all these statements—literary biographies of the more sensational modern writers, Strachey or Pound, for example, still sell well enough to be written by freelance writers for trade publishers—but unlike other academic subjects, economics, say, or biology, the extramural base of literature is slight. It is also of negligible importance since almost no one outside the university reads the art novel and the poetry of our time, or believes that they have any bearing on the serious business of the world. Only in the Third World, Latin America, Africa, and Asia, do the novel and poetry have something like the cultural power they exercised in the West as recently as two or three generations ago. The cultural lag of the Third World can be measured by the fact that the enraged Ayatollah Khomeini thought that a novel constituted such a serious sacrilege against Islam that the sons of the Prophet should be instructed to kill the blasphemous author Salman Rushdie.

Because of the present concentration of literary activity in departments of literature, their continuance and health in the university setting is of critical importance to literature. Literary people tend to think, despite the evidence, that literature is of crucial importance to society and take its presence in the university curriculum for granted. But as a history of literary education, of which this book is a part, has developed in recent years, it has surprised many to learn that literature, in the modern sense of vernacular literatures like French and English, not the study of rhetoric or the Greek and Latin classics, appeared as a standard subject in the university curriculum only about one hundred years ago. Charles Perrault proposed an academy in France with a belles lettres section covering grammar, eloquence, and poetry as early as 1666, but English literature made only fitful appearances here and there in the academic world until the early nineteenth century. It appeared at first in the educational margins in such places as the dissenting academies, women's extension education, mechanics' institutes, and in the Scottish and later the red-brick universities. The first professors of something like modern literature were eighteenth-century Scottish academics, Adam Smith, for a short time, and Hugh Blair, a professor of rhetoric and belles lettres at Edinburgh in 1762, usually accorded the modest honor of being the first professor of English literature. The University of London with its utilitarian mission was a center from its founding in the 1820s for the study of the history and literature of the native language, and elsewhere in the red- and white-bricks vernacular literature became a kind of "poor man's classics" associated with such broadly democratic nineteenth-century movements as utilitarianism, evangelicalism, and uplift. It was also connected with improving and civilizing the new proletariat and the growing number of urban poor seeking betterment.

Nationalism, too, played its part in pushing literature into the educational system, for during the nineteenth century it became increasingly the mark of a great people and a great language to have produced a great literature, the older the better. *Beowulf* with its seventh- or eighth-century date (recently revised to circa 1000) gave the English a distinct advantage over the Germans, who were, to their chagrin, never able to claim anything quite so early.

Literature left the educational margins and came into the standard curriculum during the transformation in the latter nineteenth century of the old-style colleges with their primary emphasis on training the individual, particularly prospective clergymen, and forming moral character, into the new Germanic type of universities. These latter were the forerunners of the modern multiversity, with their emphasis on *wissenschaft*, research and the discovery of knowledge, organized into fields of specialization and administered within separate departments. The sciences provided the epistemological model that in the new universities ruled not only hard "bench" subjects like chemistry and physics but also the soft social sciences and the even softer humanities like literature. Genuine subjects, those worthy of being taught as knowledge in a modern university, had to meet scientific requirements. The object of study had to be precisely located and analyzed according to a set methodology of objective investigation. The process eventuated in an ability to state the abstract laws lying behind and governing the phenomena.

The older English and American colleges have never fully made or been sure they wanted to make the transition to the German scientific model. At Harvard, Yale, and Princeton, as at Oxford and to a lesser degree at Cambridge, the undergraduate college remains the tail that wags the dog, and almost everywhere in the English-speaking world, college sports like rowing and football that are believed to form character remain more central to the university than the department of physics. American institutions like the Johns Hopkins University, Cornell, and the University of Chicago, founded in the later nineteenth century, were designed from the beginning, however, to be primarily scientific institutions emphasizing graduate and professional over undergraduate education. It was in this type of institution that the modern curriculum took shape, history, politics, economics, philology, and the national literatures, as well as the biological and physical sciences.

If a specific date and event are wanted for the plenary institutionalization of English literature in the academy, it could reasonably and usefully be said to be the establishment of an Honors School in English Literature at Oxford. Professors and departments of English appeared at about this same time, in the last quarter of the nineteenth century, in the leading American universities and colleges, though it was not until well into the twentieth century that Cambridge offered a degree in English literature. At Oxford, the first attempt to get English literature into the curriculum was made in 1887, and when this failed, a second successful effort was made in 1894.

The proponents of a school of literature, the most active of whom was the Victorian man of letters John Churton Collins, who made the cause his own, were Arnoldian believers in the civilizing mission of literary high culture. Matthew Arnold himself was uneasy about the proposed school, largely because he felt that it might reduce the importance of a classical education, but other literary people like John Morley were clear "that the systematic study of English literature in its widest sense would be a valuable addition to the course of university education." For Morley, as for many others, literature meant "not merely words and form, philology and style, but the contents of important writings in their relation to human thought and feeling, and the leading facts of human life and society."

When it came to argument in Convocation at Oxford, those who argued for the inclusion of the study of literature in the university were under the necessity of demonstrating that the subject could be organized and taught in a way that met scientific requirements. The harder-headed members of the faculty assumed that literature could be taught in a systematic fashion only if it were conceived of as a study of the history of language, but this was not at all what its defenders wanted literature to mean. The painful direction that the discussion took is indicated by an article in the London *Times*, May 18, 1887.

> The question of literature *versus* philology was at the bottom of the whole discussion, which consisted largely of philological disquisitions on languages and their relations. On the proposal of Mr. Snow and Mr. York Powell, Swedish, Danish, and Icelandic,

and on the proposal of Mr. Evans and Mr. York Powell, "Letto-Slavic," were added to the subjects of the school. It was carried by a large majority (60 to 11) that the examination in English should include Anglo-Saxon, and by a smaller majority (58 to 26) that English as well as German should necessitate Gothic. The proposal of Mr. Butler that literature, including such knowledge of history as may be needed for the understanding of the subject, shall have the greater (instead of equal) weight in the distribution of honours was strongly opposed by Professor Freeman. . . . Mr. Butler's amendment was rejected by 60 votes to 15.

Knowledge is real and true in scientific institutions only when it can be taught and graded in examinations, and the defenders of literature, even after accepting the study of Swedish, Danish, Icelandic, and Letto-Slavic, with examinations in Anglo-Saxon and Gothic, as well as the Greek and Latin required at that time of all undergraduates, were not able to satisfy their critics as to what kind of examinations they would give. The Regius Professor of Modern History since 1884, Edward Augustus Freeman, who was notably hostile to literature, made clear what he considered a real examination in a piece in the London *Times*, June 8, 1887. "There are many things fit for a man's personal study, which are not fit for University examinations. One of these is 'literature'. . . . [We are told] that it 'cultivates the taste, educates the sympathies, enlarges the mind'. Excellent results, against which no one has a word to say. Only we cannot examine in tastes and sympathies. The examiner, in any branch of knowledge, must stick to the duller range of that 'technical and positive information.'" Freeman had anticipated that the study of English literature would illustrate the development of the language, and when he learned that this was not the case, it was not at all evident to him or to others just what exactly English literature was or what could or should be taught about it. His famous remark in Convocation got right to the heart of the matter: "What is meant by distinguishing literature from language if by literature [is] meant study of great books, and not mere chatter about Shelley?" The attitude behind the famous remark appears in a letter to a member of Parliament of May 22, 1887:

> I hope you take some interest in our doings. We have both the Modern Language statute and the Bodleian lending question. As far as I can see, everybody who uses books wishes to have them out. . . . As for the Language statute, do you know anything about these "literary" folk, what they mean and what they want? How is it a "fraud upon letters" that a Language statute should be a Language statute? And what do they mean by "letters" and "literature" apart from language? I suppose, as I said, they want "chatter about Shelley." I told them that we did not want to discuss "the Harriet [Westbrook-Shelley] question" having enough to do with Helen, Theodora, and Mary Stewart.

The ponderous learned antifeminist joke with which the piece ends gives an idea of Freeman's real feelings, and though he was not himself in favor of introducing the sciences into liberal education at Oxford, he had a thoroughly scientific conception of how a subject of instruction should be organized, and the defenders of literature, nonplussed by the question which has haunted literary studies ever since—"what do they mean by 'letters' and 'literature' apart from language?"—were unable to satisfy his concerns. He joined with the rest of the faculty to vote down the proposal.

In response to the disappointment, Collins wrote an extremely interesting but by now almost totally forgotten book, *The Study of English Literature* (1891), showing how the study of the English literary classics could be systematic, methodical, and detailed without resort to philology. He offered sample examination questions, quite good ones, spelled out the structure of a literary course of study, and described the way in which literary history would be developed and how English literature would be tied closely to a study of its parent, the classical literatures, and its cousins, modern European literature. Collins's book should still command respect, for it anticipates in a remarkable way much of what was later done, or at least attempted, in the best departments of literature. But it was in vain. When the defenders of teaching literature came back in 1893–94, they had accepted Freeman's view that "the study of great books" could not be "mere chatter about Shelley" and therefore had to be, as Freeman assumed, the study of language. Collins, in a fit of depression, killed himself some years later.

Literary study at Oxford, and elsewhere, thus became and remained for a long time a branch of philology, based firmly on the study of dead languages which surely needed to be taught and certainly could be examined in. Few arrive speaking Letto-Slavic or pick it up casually along the way. Tracking vowel shifts, vocabulary changes, and developments of idiom, grammar, and orthography provided literary study for a time with the necessary scientific credentials, but there was from the beginning intense dissatisfaction with this conception of literature. The first Oxford professor of English literature, Sir Walter Raleigh, remarked in exasperation that studying literature had become little more than hunting sound changes through primitive Germanic forests. Before escaping to become the historian of the Royal Air Force, Raleigh became remarkably bitter about teaching literature at Oxford. A letter of his of October 12, 1914, to W. Macneile Dixon about setting grades for some students who had just taken Schools, confirms not only the darker suspicions of feminists about what has been going on in universities but Freeman's worst fears about examinations in English literature:

> ———— is a well-educated, sawdusty chap, a second will do him no harm. Miss ———— is a half-educated bright girl, with a weakness for philosophic jargon. A First will probably convince her that she is simply The Thing. But do as you like. If only one

is to be saved (and ———— would certainly misconceive his util-
ity if he got a First) it seems hard not to save the girl.

The Age of Chivalry is dead, but a father who is a bore isn't
the canker in a family that a mother who is a bore is. Just let
that be remembered. I am sorry to say it, but in my opinion Miss
———— if she gets a First, will be a bore for some years at least.
Of course the War improves her chances of recovery.

Even those like Churton Collins who rejected the philological approach to literary studies recognized that if literature were to be "a
subject of teaching," it had to meet scientific standards to at least
some degree, or, as he said again and again, be "systematized," and
"methodized," which meant for him historicized, periodized, rhetori-
cized. About the critical importance of organization to literary study,
romantic though he may have been in other ways, he had no doubts:
"Systematize a study at the universities, and it is systematized throughout the country; neglect it at those centres, and anarchy elsewhere is
the result."

Many shared this view, and as over time the study of literature
drifted away from philology, it retained academic respectability with
such semiscientific systematizing arrangements as the standard evolutionary history of literature as a cultural version of Darwinian natural
selection and development. Careful studies of the historical settings of
works of literature, textual studies establishing authentic texts, close
critical analysis of the details of the single literary work, and the other
types of literary activities still described as "research" appeared to
replicate scientific methodology in literary study. Some critics like
Roman Jakobson tried to establish the nature of "literariness" by specific linguistic tests, while I. A. Richards made literary things sound
very scientific with his images of compass needles and talk of the
satisfaction of appetencies. Northrop Frye perhaps came as close as
anyone ever got to realizing a scientific model for literature when he

called for "the assumption of total coherence" in literary study. His *Anatomy of Criticism* (1957), while positing a fundamental difference between scientific and literary study—"the search for a limiting principle in literature . . . is mistaken"—made a powerful argument for the necessity of organizing the field in a fairly tight systematic fashion: "We have to adopt the hypothesis, then, that just as there is an order of nature behind the natural sciences, so literature is not a piled aggregate of 'works,' but an order of words." Frye's own writings have been an extended attempt, scientific at least in appearance, to reveal this order by means of a "synoptic view of the scope, theory, principles, and techniques of literary criticism."

In the end it has been, sadly, more numerology than numbers, and the call for a systematic view of literature has largely fallen on deaf ears. When René Wellek in a letter to F. R. Leavis in 1937 tried to force Leavis, then the most famous and influential of the New Critics, to state precisely the grounds on which he so dictatorially declared one piece of literature good and another bad, "I could wish that you had stated your assumptions more explicitly and defended them systematically," Leavis would have none of it. He responded specifically in *The Common Pursuit*, where he said that this kind of pseudo-precision would lead to a "blunting of edge, blurring of focus, and muddled misdirection of attention: consequences of queering one discipline with the habits of another. The business of the literary critic is to attain a peculiar completeness of response and to observe a peculiarly strict relevance in developing his response into commentary." Whatever that may mean!

Gerald Graff, professor of English literature at Northwestern, in the first extensive history of the teaching of the subject in this country, *Professing Literature*, shows with a convincing analysis of all the addresses of the presidents of the Modern Language Association how literary study has over the past century lurched about, following one interest and then another, without ever coming to some coherent, con-

sistent, systematic view of itself. Graff recognizes that since literature
has no objective reality, a scientific definition is impossible, but a
working social agreement about the nature of literature and its function
has always been possible. The literary world has, however, always
moved restlessly about. For a time, literary texts were read, as decreed
at Oxford, as evidence in the history of language, then as documents
in social history, then as chapters in the biography of the writers of
the "life and times" variety. At later times, in the American new
criticism and the *Scrutiny* movement led in England by F. R. Leavis,
literature rejected its dependence on linguistics and history, and declared its autonomy as a moral and aesthetic reality existing in its
own right and providing its own special kinds of truth and understanding. Formalism has now passed in turn, and at the moment, the most
energetic types of academic literary activity—feminist, deconstructive,
new-historicist, Marxist, and psychoanalytic—share a social conception of literature described succinctly by Terry Eagleton as "modes of
feeling, valuing, perceiving and believing which have some kind of
relation to the maintenance and reproduction of social power."

Nothing in the literary field has settled down for long. Even the
critical vocabulary has remained frustratingly imprecise and vague,
so that what one critic means by a key term like *symbol* may have no
connection with its use by another. The definition of a central genre
like *tragedy* has proceeded in so many directions, many of them quirky
in the extreme, as in the end to disintegrate, rather than firm up, the
term and any experience that might possibly lie behind it. It is no
exaggeration to say that in the past century it has been possible to
believe, publish, and teach almost anything in literature that appealed
at the moment to a particular scholar, critic, or teacher.

The results have been a history of literature in the universities that
has been, in Graff's view, a lamentable educational failure made up
of endless confusion and argument, to the great detriment of the profession and the diminishment of the subject. Instead of meeting head on

and deciding the question of what literature is and does, on relative social terms if not on objective scientific grounds, literary departments have, Graff shows, settled the issues "in the time-honored way of resolving academic conflicts, by playing 'Let's Make a Deal.' The radicals will teach their pet texts and theories in their curricular enclave while the traditionalists go on humanizing away in theirs. Each faction will be protected from the criticism of the other, and the students will be spared the unseemly sight of their teachers washing their dirty linen in public. This is a good prescription for peace and quiet, but also for intellectual sterility." Professor Freeman would nod sagely and repeat his prescient words, "mere chatter about Shelley."

It was sex that, as it so often has and will in other callings of life, tested and found weakness. The modern sexual revolution, only the latest among many, began in the late 1950s and boomed in the 1960s when the Western world, having learned the dangers of denying Aphrodite from Euripides and Freud, but not the dangers of exploiting and trivializing her, began to loosen traditional restraints on sex. Sex shops and sex manuals like Alex Comfort's *Joy of Sex* and *More Joy* (the royalties from which with all the precision of poetic truth supported Robert Hutchins's think tank, the Center for the Study of Democratic Institutions, in California) appeared. Sex was consumerized. Hard and soft porn became commonplace, dial-a-porn was now available to the lonely with credit cards, magazines like *Hustler, Screw, Mouth,* and *Oz* were sold publicly in huge numbers, gay liberation fronts were formed, and a general loosening of sexual morality was openly discussed and encouraged, even practiced here and there.

In the permissive spirit of the times, the British Parliament replaced an old censorship law with the Obscene Publications Act of 1959, to the effect that even though a book might be "such as to tend to deprave and corrupt persons likely to read it," it was not subject to penalty or restraint "if it is proved that publication . . . is justified as being for the public good on the ground that it is in the interests of science,

literature, art, or learning, or of other objects of general concern."
(See Rolph for this and other quotations related to the *Chatterley* trial.)
The liberal politician Roy Jenkins, looking for a cause that would
provide him name recognition as a leader of advanced causes, showed
a hitherto unsuspected adroitness in maneuvering the act through
Parliament. The act is designed to laugh at old fuddy-duddies who
worry ridiculously about "science, literature, art, or learning" deprav-
ing or corrupting their audiences. It also enacts as law the traditional
position of romantic literature and art, from Byron to Norman Mailer,
that literature is above morality, particularly in matters of sex, and
that no limits should be placed on the artists' freedom to portray
whatever they wish, no matter how offensive to public taste or harmful
to the commonweal. Generations of writers asserted that literature
could not be pornographic by definition, only to have their claims
rejected by a society that banned their books and prosecuted them in
famous cases like that of Flaubert and *Madame Bovary* or James Joyce
and *Ulysses*. But now the artists were at last vindicated. Even if a book
tends, as the judge in the *Chatterley* trial ironically put it, "to make
morally bad, to pervert, to debase, or corrupt morally. . . . to render
morally unsound or rotten, to destroy the moral purity or chastity of
or to pervert or ruin a good quality, to debase, to defile," the Jenkins
Act protected it as a sacred form of writing, capable, like scripture,
of handling the taboo without defilement or danger.

Encouraged by the Jenkins Act, Penguin Books brought out an
unexpurgated edition of D. H. Lawrence's novel *Lady Chatterley's
Lover,* written not long before the author's death in 1929 but not
published in Britain until 1960, when Penguin printed 200,000
copies, though their usual print run was only 40,000 or 50,000.
Though the reason for publishing the novel was said to be to assert
the freedom of art, Penguin clearly expected and had big sales in this
noble cause. By 1960 the novel was well known to many, Lawrence
having become one of the great twentieth-century English literary fig-

ures, and the book having become a classic piece of high-culture soft pornography, printed in Europe and smuggled through customs by a generation avid to read about the beautiful young Lady Chatterley and her husband Sir Clifford, impotent from a war wound. Nervously unsatisfied in a gloomy great house, near the coal pits from which its wealth was dug, in the industrial north, increasingly at odds with a husband paralyzed from the waist down, bored with the smart chatter of competitive intellectuals who spend weekends there, Lady Chatterley takes a succession of lovers before finding deep Lawrencian contentment, "burning molten and soft in her womb and bowels," in the embraces of the estate's gamekeeper, Mellors.

The difficulty of getting the book printed earlier was caused by frequent and explicit descriptions of sex, including sodomy, and the plain language used in the sexual encounters. As the bold defense attorney in the case put it to the not yet knighted but already redoubtable Oxford don and leading literary critic, Miss Helen Gardner, "the word 'fuck' or 'fucking' occurs not less than thirty times. What, in your view, is the relation of the four-letter words in this book to its literary merits?"

On the face of it it is not apparent why the public prosecutor elected to charge Penguin Books with publishing an obscene work, since Lawrence's novel by then was widely established as literature and consequently protected from prosecution by the new act. Politics and class were mixed up in the matter. The Jenkins Act expressed liberal values and had been pushed by an ambitious politician and some of the more liberal members of Parliament. And the subject of this particular book, the buggering of the wife of a mutilated war hero and member of the upper classes by one of his servants, might possibly have been offensive to conservatives. But the real reason would seem to have been that there were those in the government and the legal profession, like the prosecuting attorney and the judge in the *Lady Chatterley* case, who did not accept what Parliament had done and were unwilling to allow the legalization of the principle that art takes precedence over all other values of a society to go unchallenged. The *Lady Chatterley* trial was only the first of many prosecutions of books like *Fanny Hill, Last Exit to Brooklyn, The Naked Lunch, The Little Red Schoolbook*, and others that were offensive to the more conservative.

A rightish tendency in the prosecution appeared throughout the trial, as when one witness was asked whether he would allow his wife and his servants to read *Lady Chatterley*. There was equally a leftish tinge to the defense, which accorded well with romantic literature's traditional identification with the folk and the simple things of life. Though Lawrence himself was often charged with fascism, he had begun humbly as the son of a coal miner, in Britain the mythic type of manual labor, as idealized, and subsidized, as the family farmer in America. The publisher of the book was Sir Allen Lane, head of Penguin Books, which had with a missionary zeal undertaken to publish not only *Lady Chatterley* but nearly all of Lawrence's other works, and a great many of the world's classics of literature, in paperback at the modest price of three shillings sixpence, "the price of ten cigarettes," as was said at the trial, making literature thereby available to the people. Only the poor, it should perhaps be remembered, bought cigarettes in tens, rather than twenties, at that time. Sir Allen let it drop during his testimony that he had himself "left school and started work when [he was] sixteen," and Richard Hoggart, testifying for the defense, told the court that he was "born into the working class and . . . was orphaned at the age of eight and brought up by my grandmother," a background that gave him special insight, he felt, into the free and natural use of four-letter words in ordinary life.

Whatever the political and class issues in the background, the figure in the dock at the *Lady Chatterley* trial was literature itself. The writer involved, David Herbert Lawrence, was by 1960 a literary saint, one of the supreme modern artists, declared by F. R. Leavis, the Cambridge don who was the most influential of the English critics at that time, to be one of the only three or four writers belonging to "the great tradition" of English literature. Leavis refused, however, to testify for the defense at this trial on the grounds that *Lady Chatterley* was not one of Lawrence's best works. Lawrence had died of tuberculosis, still by 1929 the authenticating disease of the true romantic artist, at an early age after years of Ovidian exile. His novels attacking the grimness of modern British industrial society and proclaiming the salvation in the emotions, particularly sex, experienced not promiscuously but in some dark and mystical force of blood, were archetypes of the essential romantic subject.

The exact legal issue was never really sorted out. At times the focus was on whether *Lady Chatterley* was obscene, and what obscenity meant. But the legal question turned on whether the novel was literature, since if it was literature, then, according to the Jenkins Act, it didn't matter whether it was obscene. It therefore was necessary to define literature in order to determine whether *Lady Chatterley* fit the specifications, and the trial became a public dramatization of the question, "What is Literature, and how does it differ from other forms of writing?" Surely the ghost of Professor E. A. Freeman must again have smiled grimly at this legal replay of the question—"What do they mean by 'letters' and 'literature'?"—he had asked in such a different moral climate at Oxford.

Once again it was the responsibility of the literary establishment, predominantly academic by now, to answer the question. Who should know better how to define literature? There were practical matters at stake. If the experts could convincingly define literature in a manner that would include *Lady Chatterley*, then not only would one of the great suppressed works of literature be fully enfranchised but one of the great tenets of romanticism and modernism, the superiority of art to morality and middle-class values, would be justified. The trial had its symbolic aspect as well, an opportunity to display to the world the existence and the importance of literature in the social order. All the right people for the job were there, a panorama of those who write, teach, and explain literature, almost always with some university connection. There were distinguished writers, E. M. Forster, C. Day Lewis, Dame Rebecca West, Richard Hoggart, and Stephen Potter. Prominent critics and university teachers who had lectured and written on Lawrence, like Graham Hough, Kenneth Muir, Helen Gardner, Raymond Williams, Joan Bennett. Public men of letters like Noel Annan, Sir William Emrys Williams, Norman St. John-Stevas. Cultured churchmen like the bishop of Woolwich, cultivated politicians like Roy Jenkins, M.P., and a host of others, some thirty-five in all, ending with Miss Bernardine Wall, a recent graduate of Cambridge, now writing a novel, who had recently read, twice, an unexpurgated copy of *Lady Chatterley* and found it artistically much superior to the expurgated version she had read as a schoolgirl.

Here was the literary establishment centered in the university, the institution itself made visible—authors and savants, public-spirited publishers and broad-minded clerics, public men of letters and intellectuals—testifying solemnly on the linked questions "What is literature?" and "Is *Lady Chatterley* literature?" These matters were sometimes approached in social terms. In an attempt to establish at once that the novel was indeed literature, Professor Vivian De Sola Pinto of Nottingham University, where Lawrence had once attended, was asked had *Lady Chatterley* been included in an exhibition at the university? was the book in the university library? were students encouraged to read it? and was it included in the examination for the honor's degree? (Still the shade of Professor Freeman!) Encouraged by positive answers to all these questions, Gerald Gardiner, Q.C., the lawyer for the defense, went on to ask about the translation and publication of Lawrence's works in other countries: "How far is the fact that the novels of an English author have been published in most other Western countries an indication of the literary merits of the book?"

Professor De Sola Pinto agreed that it was "one indication," and then added hastily that it was "a certain sign." But he wanted to make it clear that "literariness" was finally in the gift of his own profession: "I suppose a surer criterion . . . of literary merit would be if [the novels] were studied in the universities and prescribed by the people who teach in the universities."

Working in this way, it was slowly established that literature is the kind of writing that is written by an author of acknowledged genius, that it consists of the books that are taught in university literary programs, and that it is the books recognized as literature by those professionals who write it, judge it, describe it, teach it, and write books about it. Dame Rebecca West, long a professional writer, phrased the social definition somewhat more firmly than directly, "The great literary merit of [Lawrence's] book is something that readers accord by reading him in such large numbers, and his critics accord by writing so much about him." But, struck by a second thought, she added, "it is not an easy matter to define the literary merit."

The waters might have remained clearer if this kind of sociological definition of literature—is Lawrence taught and read and examined in the literary course of study?—had prevailed, but inevitably the experts, encouraged by their brief moment in the light of a public courtroom, ventured into the deeps where essential qualities of literature are believed to lurk. Sometimes the definition involved formal characteristics of the literary work, sometimes it was a matter of authorial intention, sometimes of tone and content. Richard Hoggart thought *Lady Chatterley* "a book of quite exceptional literary merit," because "the overwhelming impression which comes out to me as a careful reader of it is of the enormous reverence which must be paid by one human being to another with whom he is in love and, in particular, the reverence towards one's physical relationships." For Helen Gardner the literary standard was less sentimental and more rhetorical:

> I think in discussing literary merit one has to give weight to two things. One is, I think, what the writer is trying to say, and the other is his success in saying it. These two are not always commensurate. One can find great literary merit in a piece of writing of a trivial experience of great importance and great value, although one may feel at times the writer has not wholly succeeded in communicating what he wishes to communicate. I think [the questionable passages in *Lady Chatterley*] do succeed, far beyond expectation, in doing something extraordinarily difficult, which very few other writers have really attempted with such courage and devotion, and that is to attempt to put into words experiences that are really very difficult to verbalize.

Whether some subjects are appropriate for literature, while others are not, the ugly as well as the beautiful, is an old question in aesthetics, and it came up frequently in the court, usually in relation to the rough sex and rougher language in the novel. The judge, believing that "dirt" could not be art, put it directly to Dame Rebecca West, "What is the literary merit of this book?" She waffled at first, but drew herself together in time to insist that literature could treat of any subject so long as it did so seriously and well.

> *Lady Chatterley's Lover* is full of sentences of which any child could make a fool, because they are badly written. He was a man with no background of formal education in his home. He also had a great defect which mars this book. He had absolutely no sense of humour. A lot of pages in this book are, to my point of view, ludicrous, but I would still say this is a book of undoubted literary merit. After all, a work of art is not an arbitrary thing. A work of art is an analysis of an experience, and a synthesis of the findings of the analysis, that makes life a serious matter and makes the world seem beautiful. And though there are ugly things, though there is this unsuccessful attempt to handle the ugly words, this is still from that standard a good book in my opinion.

Graham Hough was a bit more straightforward but little more precise. To the prosecution's hopeful ground-clearing question, "Will you tell us as an expert in English literature what are the matters which ought to be taken into account in assessing the literary merits of a book?" he responded, "I think that's a very difficult thing to do in general terms, and I think it varies very much with the kind of book it is. We are here discussing a novel, and I think one of the things one would wish to take into account is whether it is a true and sincere representation of an aspect of life. . . . the book is concerned with a very important situation; it is concerned with the relations of men and women, with their sexual relations, with the nature of marriage, and these are all matters of deep importance to all of us."

Aware perhaps that this was a trifle vague, Hough sharpened his definition by adding that it was most important for literature that the characters should be "extremely closely and intimately drawn."

Literature was also defined as a special type of historical writing that preserved ways people thought and felt in the past and made them available to the present. Offered this opening, the prosecution charged through the gap to ask expert witnesses whether Lawrence offered an accurate picture of his time and its manners. When he was assured that this was very much the case, he scored some points by calling attention to the disastrous scene in the novel where Lady Chatterley's father, a distinguished painter and member of the Royal Academy, takes Mellors the gamekeeper to lunch at his club. There over a few drinks the two men chuckle away about screwing, the painter reminisces about his own sexual conquests, and digs the gamekeeper in the ribs, laughing with him about Mellors's success in impregnating Lady Chatterley. On reflection, no one defended this as a historically accurate picture of clubs or RAs of former times.

The *Lady Chatterley* trial took place, of course, in 1960, before the high age of literary theory arrived and academics became more self-conscious about poetics. But after all allowances are made, the explanations of literary matters offered to the court by the expert witnesses from the literary departments of the universities are embarrassingly confused and contradictory, dog-eared really, and so vague and awkwardly expressed as to suggest that no careful thought had gone into them, which it had not. The deficiencies are nowhere more glaringly apparent than in what was said about the formal characteristics of literary texts. Mervyn Griffith-Jones, the four-square Welsh prosecuting attorney whom Jenkins called "that indefatigable scourge of the impure," was, or at least pretended to be, not very literary. He spoke of the magazine funded by the CIA *The Encounter*, rather than *Encounter*, drawing a wan, knowing smile, of the kind used by those who have much to put up with, from its editor, Stephen Spender, who was sitting in court among other cognoscenti tittering at the lawyer's solecism. He blustered at Graham Hough: "Would you agree with me that a good book by a good writer, generally speaking, should not repeat things again and again? It is a tiresome habit, is it not?" Hough: "No, I do not agree with this. There is a great deal of this in the Bible, for instance. Repetition is very frequently employed." Griffith-Jones had earlier spoken of Lawrence's misquoting the Bible, presumably knowing it well and approving of it, and so Hough would seem to have smote him hip and thigh. But however often he had read and heard the sonorous parallelisms of the King James version, Griffith-Jones had apparently never before encountered anything like the Lawrencian unwillingness to leave anything before saying it at least six or eight times, and he would not let it go. "Do you regard that as good writing, to repeat again and again 'womb and bowels,' 'womb and bowels,' and 'bowels and womb?' . . . Is that really what you call expert, artistic writing?" To which Hough could only gamely reply, "He always writes like that, and he brings it off." The same question of repetitiveness as a literary quality came up again in consideration of whether the sex scenes are simply the same thing over and over again, except for changes of setting, and whether this detracts from the literary merit of the book.

Along with other elements of literary style, metaphors, those primary tropes of romantic literature, got a careful scrutiny. Griffith-Jones: "Can one flow and be alive in one's womb and bowels?"—"Metaphorically I think one can." "Even metaphorically?"—"Yes." Structure, too, comes in for consideration, and there was much discussion about whether "the introduction of irrelevant matter would detract from the literary merit of a book." Since the orthodox answer was, at least at that time when formalism was still dominant, "Yes," then it became a matter of importance whether Lawrence's novel is tightly assembled or whether the main story is no more than an excuse for the sex scenes. In the opinion of the experts a true work of literature had to be taken as a whole, which evoked a meandering and footless discussion of whether the nonsexual parts of the book, all those coal mines and midlands' discussions of art, had any literary purpose. These questions in turn led on to the loose way in which the novel was written. In his usual way, Lawrence had written three versions, but the version known as *The First Lady Chatterley*, did not contain the explicit sexual scenes and language, which were added to the later versions, and might therefore be suspected of having been added more to promote sales than to enhance art. Lawrence did in fact publish an expensive edition of the enhanced version in Florence, which made quite a lot of money.

This is all pretty dim—but then the British literary establishment had never made its stand on the ground of abstract theory. Morality was their meat, and it was on moral grounds, felt more deeply than rationalized, that the establishment defended Lawrence, *Lady Chatterley*, and literature. In doing so they were explicit that they were not defending promiscuity or obscenity, protesting that both they and Lawrence would have none of these vulgarities. Nor did they really care very much for sex at the physical level of fluids and friction, or for the rough language Lawrence had used to express carnal excitement and raw sexual energy. It is, in fact, hard not to feel in reading the testimony of the literary experts that for all their goodwill, theirs were exactly, precisely, the kind of over-intellectualized and moralized responses to sex and to art that Lawrence ridiculed in *Lady Chatterley*. Their position was that Lawrence and his high art had transmuted what would otherwise be ugly and despicable, namely rough sex, into transcendent literature. Dame Rebecca West, and who seemingly better qualified, glimpsed for a brief moment that Lawrence might have been after "a return of the soul to the more intense life," but then, with a return of the qualities that must have once made H. G. Wells wonder what he had gotten into, she felt required to add that the emotion Lawrence sought to portray must have been something "felt when people had had a different culture, such as the cultural basis of religious faith."

One of the liberal clerics who testified for the defense found the novel intensely moral in that it makes us know that God is not only love but sexual love: "God himself is a creator, . . . man shares in the responsibility for creation, and that . . . is directly expressed in the relationship of the sexes." Though *Lady Chatterley* is a story of adultery, some of the experts proclaimed it a defense of marriage, "true marriage," of course, while others pronounced it not only fit for their own children and those of others but moral in the deepest sense of Christian ethics, a "right and wholesome view of sex," ideal for use as a tract for underprivileged youth groups, said one, a portrayal of stable relationships, a defense of chastity against promiscuity and pornography, said others. Instead of accepting what Lawrence shouts from the housetop again and again and again, that *fucking* is good and that it is the only thing that can save people from a world gone mad with rationality, the litterateurs, with all the ingenious perversity of intellectuals having to say *something*, turned the book on its head. For Richard Hoggart, Lawrence was a puritan, which he was in a strange quirky modern kind of way, going on about the one and only acceptable orgasm and the frigidity of women, and *Lady Chatterley* was "puritanical in its reverence" for life, an act, in the words of a mitred bishop, "of holy communion."

Here, in the *Lady Chatterley* trial, the literary subculture made the case for literary art in the public forum of the court. Griffith-Jones, the prosecutor, was unimpressed. He kept his feet firmly on the ground, refusing to cross-examine most of the witnesses called by the defense, standing up only to bedevil the more tempting of them, and producing no witnesses of his own. His explanation was that he accepted the literary merit of the book, which should have legally been the end of the matter. But he still felt the novel to be deeply immoral and insisted throughout, despite the clear sense of the statute, that obscenity and morality were the real issues.

Mr. Justice Byrne, the presiding judge, felt the same way, only more strongly. His legal instructions to the jury sagely advised them not to "allow yourselves to get lost in the higher realms of literature." He went on to direct their attention to just how one might get lost: "You will no doubt ask yourselves whether, unless a person was a student of literature, an authority on English literature, and a student of Lawrence, he would be able to read into this book the many different things that many of these witnesses have said he intended should be in the book." Whatever Parliament and bishops and literary people might say, in the end for Mr. Justice Byrne, not art but "morality is fundamental to the well-being of the community." Of course, Judge Byrne acknowledged,

> there is a right to express oneself, either in pictures or in literature. People who hold strong political views are often anxious to say exactly what they think, irrespective of any restraint, and so too a creative writer or a creative artist, one can well understand, naturally desires complete freedom within which to express his talents or his genius. But he is a member of the

community like any other member of the community. He is under the same obligation to other members of the community as any other is, not to do harm, either mentally or physically or spiritually, and if there is a conflict between an artist or writer in his desire for self-expression, and the sense that morality is fundamental to the well-being of the community, if there is such a conflict, then it is morality that must prevail.

Literary people avoided the real question, but the judge did not. Art, the judge said in his old-fashioned downright way is the servant of society, not the privileged visitant from another higher realm of being as romanticism and modernism had claimed, as the universities had taught, and as Parliament had now made the law. But though the judge refused to order that the defense's legal expenses be paid, the jury found for Penguin Books, and the publisher went on to sell over two million copies of the unexpurgated *Lady Chatterley* in the first year of publication. Roy Jenkins became a famous liberal politician and chancellor of Oxford University, Sir Allen Lane became a millionaire. Literature did not fare so well.

The *Lady Chatterley* case was, of course, little more than a momentary scandal, more a media event than a historical event of any importance. Many literary people were intensely embarrassed by it, Dame Edith Sitwell and Katherine Anne Porter, for two, believing that it simply confirmed the world in its conviction that literature is a naïve business, and those connected professionally with it both venal and silly. John Sparrow in an article in *Encounter* mocked the solemnities of the testimony by pointing out that those who were praising Lawrence's sex as a "reverence for life" were completely unaware that Mellors on at least one occasion was sodomizing Lady Chatterley.

But the inability of the literary professionals in the *Lady Chatterley* case to describe with any precision and concert the characteristics of literature or to state with any firmness and conviction its place in social life is symptomatic of a larger historical failure to inscribe literature very deeply in the culture. Lévi-Strauss's structural anthropology has demonstrated, particularly in *The Savage Mind*, that in primitive cultures, kinship or religion, or any other social structure, becomes firm and real only when it is elaborately systematized. Failure to build up values or concepts on binary principles, along paradigmatic and syntagmatic axes, into full-scale plausible theories leaves institutional practices without necessary social foundations. This same necessity prevails no less in modern Western society, where science provides the basic model for the required theory. What the *Lady Chatterley* case showed so dramatically was literature's lack of any theoretical basis, any systematic organization of its parts in a way that makes it real and meaningful to the eyes of the beholder and in the social world at large. The faintness of its cultural existence is obvious, and the inability of the literary experts in the *Lady Chatterley* case to define literature makes clear why this is the case. It is in the university, however, that the consequences of the lack of system have become most distinctly visible.

When literature was admitted to the modern university as a form of knowledge, it entered into an unwritten contract, some might say a Faustian bargain, to conform to the governing standards of knowledge, which were then and still are set by science. It agreed, that is, to define its object of study with some precision, develop a standard analytical methodology, and determine literature's functions. Nothing like the elaborate structures of modern chemistry or physics was ever required, for it has been generally understood that different subjects are capable of different degrees of systematization. It would have been enough, for example, to agree on and develop what many in fact do believe to be the case, that literature is probably best described as fiction. It might have been necessary to add that it is a self-conscious fiction in order to distinguish it from those other types of fictional discourse like philosophy and history that insist on their responsibility to facts and their own factuality. Or it could have equally well been said, again with wide agreement, that, as distinct from subjects that treat life in terms of the statistical norm, say, sociology and anthropology, literature portrays various aspects of existence as they are experienced by individuals. Sir Walter Raleigh early on perfectly grasped the issue, and the failure to deal with it, "The first problem for a writer is 'Why write anything?' it's there that we stick. Universities accept and encourage appallingly inadequate answers to this question."

There are those, like Stéphane Mallarmé and T. S. Eliot, for example, who have believed that any attempts to teach literature in any way whatsoever have been not only misguided but destructive. And there have been many others, most famously F. R. Leavis, who have thought that any attempt to systematize literary study was the merest folly, more scientism than science. The unscientific looseness of literary study, its pluralism, as it is more positively put, has been felt by many to be its strength, recently and eloquently by Wayne Booth, who has recommended and practiced at intolerable length, toleration and full understanding of all critical points of view. This kind of freedom, it has long been argued, avoids the narrowness of historical study and the pseudo-scientific dogmatism of sociology, allowing literary study to pursue a wide range of human interests and concerns in any manner that seems most rewarding and interesting. Literature, the argument goes on, is a catch-all category made up of so many different kinds of texts and so many various critical views, that it makes no sense to think of bringing it together as a single coherent subject, or to look at it from any one point of view.

This nominalism and anti-essentialism have an undeniable force, but their obvious though unquantifiable consequences in practice for literature have been a steady decrease of intellectual respectability in a university setting where true knowledge has continued to be required to meet at least something like scientific standards. The decay is most immediately visible in the steady decrease in the past twenty years of enrollments and majors in literature in the United States. There are, of course, other reasons for this decrease than the inability to explain what literature is and why it is important, but in a time of trial literature has only feebly justified itself, and in most places literature departments have decayed into service departments providing support work in reading and writing skills for the least qualified students.

The theoretical naïveté and innocence of system displayed by the literary establishment in the *Lady Chatterley* trial left it always vulnerable, and during and after the 1960s structuralist and poststructuralist theorists with strong political interests were able to get at and demolish the old literary order through this weakness. Partly Protestant Reformation and partly French Revolution, the critical revolution swept through literary studies like measles through a primitive tribe, demonstrating with ease the emptiness of the old literary order, demystifying and "emptying out" its unsupported humanistic beliefs.

3

Authors as Rentiers,

Readers as Proletariat,

Critics as Revolutionaries

Now, in the late twentieth century, we stand among the ruins of what not long ago seemed new but very rapidly became the old literary order. To date its breakdown precisely or to state the causes exactly is impossible, but a series of essays by Lionel Trilling collected as *Beyond Culture*, particularly "On the Teaching of Modern Literature" (1961) and "The Two Environments: Reflections on the Study of English" (1965), record how the changes came to and were experienced by the defenders of what had until then seemed so advanced, liberal, and even radical, and now had suddenly, to their surprise, become a literary ancien régime. Trilling not only provides a description of what happened and offers an explanation of why it happened but conveys just how confusing and painful the change was.

The attack on literature first began to be noticeable in the universities in the disturbances connected with the Vietnam War, such as the free-speech movement in California in the early 1960s, the student revolt in the streets of Paris in 1968, and the disruptions that peaked at Columbia, where Trilling taught, late in that decade. The attack was not at first pointed directly at literature but more generally at the universities, including all their departments and subjects of instruction, as a vulnerable part of the power structure. Trilling, who by then was the public figure best representing academic letters in America, understood, however, that there was a close connection between these events and literature. A critic in the tradition of Matthew Arnold, whose biography he had written and whose reasonable style of writing and argument had remained his model, he had always been a spokesman for the social and moral values of literature and literary criticism.

The essays in *Beyond Culture*, to the profound shock of the literary community, far from defending high culture against what was viewed as the oncoming of barbarism, expressed responsibility for the situation and went on to voice the gravest doubts about the usefulness of teaching literature in the universities. It was particularly modern literature, Kafka, Joyce, Mann, Eliot, that troubled Trilling. He had been instrumental in introducing these writings earlier into the curriculum at Columbia, with the optimistic belief that their alienated attitudes would shock middle-class students with unenquiring conventional ways of thinking into an Arnoldian "free play of mind" and a consideration of "the best that is known and thought in the world." Instead, Trilling tells us, the fact of teaching modern literary works, which, despite their complexity, always had to be discussed hurriedly in the classroom, had conferred the status of classics on them, and put the stamp of authority on what they had to say, thereby encouraging easy, unquestioning acceptance rather than hard thought about the dark view of life they offered.

In the face of the anger loose on campus, Trilling belatedly and painfully had to recognize what we have seen in chapter 1, that since the late 1700s literature had its face set against the mainline social order. Acknowledging that the classics of modern literature are not politically or socially neutral, he perceived, apparently for the first time, a "bitter line of hostility to civilization which runs through

Cecilia
Dorothea
Belinda

modern literature." Joyce, Eliot, and others had helped to legitimate the subversive, to establish an ideology of alienation, which was now accepted as automatically by students as the old bourgeois truisms that modern literature had been introduced to combat. The old, mindless middle-class conventionality, Trilling now believed sadly, had given way, with modern literature's help, to a new equally mindless "adversary culture." Preferring style over ethics, barren of self-consciousness, indifferent to older writing, and given to automatic responses of negation and antagonism to all political, educational, and literary authority, the adversary culture was contemptuously hostile to what Trilling in his old-fashioned way called "civilization."

It was this adversary culture, legitimated in part by poems like *The Waste Land* and novels like *The Trial*, that in the 1960s was there in front of university administration buildings screaming "Shut the motherfucker down!" and writing graffiti like "Off the Pigs" with spray cans on the walls of libraries where the best that has been thought and said had been laboriously collected. Scenes like these so profoundly alarmed Trilling that he began, along with many others, to think and say what would not long before have been unthinkable as well as unspeakable for him. He now faced the possibility that a romantic and modernist literature that relentlessly attacked rationality and scorned an orderly world might be socially flawed in some fundamental way. A literature of alienation, Trilling found himself saying, may not always tell all the truth, and "can even generate falsehood and habituate us to it." He later described his own reaction to the situation as "a despairing shrug." His contemporaries took his response more as a failure of nerve than an anagnorisis, but his sense of what was happening and what would come of it was prophetic.

Looking back, it seems odd, naïve even, that so perceptive a social critic as Trilling had not earlier been aware of the subversive, anti-establishment ideology of literary modernism, and indeed of romantic literature as a whole. But after the literary radicalism of the Depression

1930s, anti-Stalinists like Trilling, wary of politics, had sought and claimed for literature a privilege to comment on social life while remaining above political activity. Lawrence H. Schwartz's *Creating Faulkner's Reputation: The Politics of Modern Literary Criticism* shows how Trilling and others, Malcolm Cowley most obviously, had at this time purposely sought and made the reputation of an essentially American writer who seemed apolitical and more concerned with style and craft than social commentary. Now, however, campus radicals and intellectuals were determined to politicize literature, along with all other subjects and activities, once again. It seemed to many a bit unfair, given its traditional antagonism toward middle-class society and its values, that in this new scenario literature should be cast in the role of the cultural representative of a materialistic society, but this only confirms that, as I have earlier argued, literature for all its alienated stance was all along de facto one of the high cultural institutions of liberal democracy.

The attack in the 1960s and 1970s on high culture and the universities was not as violent as the cultural revolution then being made by the Red Guards in the People's Republic of China. It confined itself largely to the safety of the campuses, creating what W. V. Quine described as "a modest but viable terror [that] sufficed, in the event, to bring universities to their knees." There was more violence in the streets of Paris and in the German universities than in most American universities. The literary days of rage got no further here than a modest *coup d'hôtel* at an annual meeting of the Modern Language Association in the winter of 1968 where a group of young radicals took over the stodgiest and least political of all professional associations. It was an intellectual rather than a street revolution that dismantled the old literary order. Literary criticism was the chief weapon, and the revolution proceeded in much the same way as the philosophes had in discrediting the mysteries of the ancien régime.

Literary criticism is one of those many human activities that flourish like the green bay tree without anyone ever being able precisely to say what they are or what might be their function, probably because they have so many different functions, and these change over time. Criticism traditionally has aspired to be the science of literary discourse, standing to literature as physics does to nature. This is the position that Cleanth Brooks and W. K. Wimsatt claimed for criticism in their standard history of criticism: "The first principle on which we would insist is that of continuity and intelligibility in the history of literary argument. Plato has a bearing on Croce and Freud, and vice versa. Or, all three of these theorists are engaged with a common reality and hence engage one another through the medium of that reality and either come to terms or disagree. Literary problems occur not just because history produces them, but because literature is a thing of such and such a sort, showing a relation to the rest of human experience."

Anthologies of literary criticism make the same point implicitly by offering a selection of criticism extending from Plato to the present, as if criticism had a continuous history. But these volumes regularly include, particularly in the older periods, pieces of philosophy, rhetoric, theology, and other kinds of writing that are styled literary criticism in order to make it appear that criticism is a natural and inevitable human activity, practiced continuously from antiquity to the present. A chronological analysis of one of these typical anthologies of criticism, Hazard Adams—*Critical Theory since Plato*—shows, however, that the history of criticism has been anything but continuous: thirty items in the millennia before Kant, thirty-two from Kant to Croce, forty-six since Croce.

With a few earlier exceptions like Aristotle's *Poetics* and Horace's *Ars Poetica*, criticism when it is looked at in a historical context became a standard literary genre only in the eighteenth century, when print made letters into a business. Boileau in the later seventeenth century was the first systematic critic in France, and Samuel Johnson pronounced in his life of Dryden that that writer "may be properly considered as the father of English criticism, as the writer who first taught us to determine upon principles the merit of composition. Of our former poets, the greatest dramatist [Shakespeare] wrote without rules, conducted through life and nature by a genius that rarely misled, and rarely deserted him. Of the rest, those who knew the laws of propriety had neglected to teach them."

After its formalization as a standard literary mode in the late seventeenth and early eighteenth centuries, the critical impulse was used for a host of mundane tasks, such as advertising and reviewing the new books pouring from the press, improving the taste of the new common readers, and providing expert judgments about literary questions. In its later as well as its earlier phases, it has been not so much a science of literature as a provider of the various institutional services—accommodation, assimilation, apology, interpretation, legitimation, formation of ideology, cosmicization, and so on—needed to keep literature plausible and functional in changing social circumstances. The bulge in criticism since about the time of Croce, for example, correlates precisely with the appearance of literature in the university curriculum in the late nineteenth century and the consequent need of professors to conduct "research" and to publish "original contributions to knowledge."

Poets, in the largest sense of that term, as "makers" and "creators" in all artistic genres, have remained, at least until recently, the aristocrats of literature, scorning the base critic, who has had to kiss the rod of creative genius. Momos, the persistent fault-finder of classical literature, returned in the eighteenth century as the image of the modern critic, and Swift, horrified by the appearance of this critical monster, portrayed its birth in *The Battle of the Books* in the terms that Milton used in *Paradise Lost* for the incestuous coupling of Satan with Sin to beget Death. As the bourgeois professional selling services to literature at best, at worst the menial servant of literature, doing all the odd jobs around the institution required to keep things working—reviews of literary works, critical essays, literary histories, concordances, editions of literary texts, interpretation of texts for the classroom, etc., etc.—criticism has remained in an inferior, really not quite respectable status in the literary hierarchy during most of its brief life. "The formal discourse of an amateur," R. P. Blackmur, not a particularly humble man, humbly called it. "Criticism is not autonomous," he went on, and after it has said all it can, "there will always remain, quite untouched, the thing itself," the thing being the pure work of literary art, crystalline, removed, autonomous. Even that model of the critic, Matthew Arnold, himself a poet, of course, admitted "the inherent superiority of the creative effort of the human spirit over its critical effort." Eliot, a poet with high aristocratic tastes, was particularly adept at making academic critics feel their inferiority, as in the following passage from "The Function of Criticism," where he speaks of them in the tone of tired exasperation of a busy man who has at last been compelled to pay attention to unsatisfactory tradesmen: "The critic's task . . . appears to be quite clearly cut out for him; and it ought to be comparatively easy to decide whether he performs it satisfactorily, and in general, what kinds of criticism are useful and what are otiose. But on giving the matter a little attention, we perceive that criticism, far from being a simple and orderly field of beneficent activity, from which impostors can be readily ejected, is no better than a Sunday park of contending and contentious orators, who have not even arrived at the articulation of their differences."

The critics, first the Victorian men of letters and then mostly the professors of literature in the universities, proud and ambitious men and, now, women, have been determinedly upwardly mobile, regularly recruited, in fact, from socioeconomic groups trying desperately to better themselves, first the poor Wasp boys from Manchester and North Platte, then the Irish, the Italians, and the Jews, now women, blacks, and Third World groups. From the beginning there have been attempts at making critics seem more necessary and important. The very social Henry James, for example, in *The Art of Fiction* (1884), trying to justify the seriousness of the complex novels he wrote, made the case for the need for criticism to heighten the reality of literature. Times when literature is not *"discutable"* are likely to be dull, James said, for the novel "must take itself seriously for the public to take it so." Arnold too insisted that there are times when *only* criticism is possible, because there are times, like the romantic period, in his view, when the poets "did not know enough" and needed critics to sort out the intellectual world for them.

Literary critics, Richard Ohman shows us, have most effectively and consistently sought to improve their social status by becoming, as practitioners of medicine had earlier, and of dentistry and insurance soon would, members of a profession. Professionalization is the means by which the middle-class historically has dignified the way it earns a living in the face of aristocratic and high-bourgeois disdain for work and profit. Professions establish that they offer something, health in the case of medicine, for example, justice in law, that society vitally needs, and that members of the profession offer in a disinterested fashion, that is, without regard for money or self-advancement. Long professional training, not apprenticeship, is required for a professional to acquire what is finally more of an art than a skill. The experts created by this long training know better than their clients what is best for them and are under no obligation, indeed it would be counterproductive, to explain theories and practices to those they treat. The doctor owes the patient no description of either the disease or the proposed course of treatment. Professions, finally, require the construction over time of a legitimating body of theory, baffling to the layman because written in technical terms known only to the professional. A dead language like Latin serves best, arcane mathematical symbols work well, too; an obscure, repetitious, and jargon-ridden criticism has had to serve literature.

The history of literature in the universities during the last century, according to Ohman, follows step by step the standard pattern for transforming work to a profession. Far from being even a rudimentary science of literature, the huge growth of literary scholarship and criticism that has taken place in the past century, for example, was actually only "a mystification . . . conceal[ing] the true relationship of things," but it supplied the body of specialized material, of interest to and understood only by specialists, if by them, needed to establish the professional credentials of literary criticism. Tenure, departmental structures, and professional organizations made possible the ethos that relieved the professor of literature from explaining to the laity, especially the students, why English 501*, "The Early Plays of Sir Arthur Wing Pinero," and English 502*, "The Later Plays of Pinero," are both needed to satisfy the requirements for the degree of Ph.D. Graduate schools, with their long-extended course of study—eight to ten years is staunchly defended on both coasts, in Cambridge and Berkeley, and not at all unusual in other places where a pool of cheap labor is needed to teach undergraduates and keep down instructional costs—provide professional training for the recruits who, soon after developing the "right feel" for literature, join their elders in proclaiming its critical importance to the social world and the continuous sacrifice of those who selflessly provide it.

The social position of critics and criticism improved enormously by achieving professional status, but the situation remained uneasy. "Those who can't, teach." The sharp decline in the quality of novels, poems, and plays of recent years offered an opportunity for the critic to gain some ground on the author, and the "adversary culture's" attempts to seize power in the 1960s offered the occasion. Critics became more assertive than previously in insisting on the importance of their writing to literature and to society at large. Geoffrey Hartman, a scholar who chafed considerably under the necessities of keeping school—"the danger of being routinized or contaminated by endless readings forced out of the industrious hordes of students"—has argued provocatively that criticism today is at least as creative as contemporary literature (contemporary literature being in a considerably depressed state) and might well be considered a primary literary form rather than a secondary support system. Harold Bloom invented a better critical mousetrap consisting of two poetic types, the strong poet who finds his own voice and escapes the control of his predecessor, and the weak poet who can't get those who have written before him out of his head. For a time at least, the poets, no longer very robust and always anxious to be reassured about their talents, beat a path to the Bloomian door to find out whether they would be pronounced "strong" or "weak." Advertisements for new collections of poetry would proudly proclaim that R. P. Warren or A. R. Ammons had been stamped "strong poets" by Bloom.

Criticism almost single-handedly, the writers seemingly having nothing to say in the matter, turned literature around in a way that by now, whatever the consequences, is irreversible. Beforehand it would have been expected that literary criticism would have in a time of crisis such as Trilling describes played out its traditional social role of secondary legitimation, defending as much as possible the traditional views of the institution of which it is a part, even as theology adjusts religious dogma to new situations in times of danger.

What actually happened has been quite the reverse, so unexpected and out of the ordinary as to require some considerable attention. Deconstruction, the covering term increasingly used for the broad range of literary criticism that discredited the old literature, turned on literature with the strange ferocity that so bewildered Trilling and charged it with having been mystifying, illogical, and harmful rather than beneficent. "No more literature" and "the death of literature" were the rallying words of literary radicals who were not philistines but themselves intellectuals, students, and teachers, usually working in the universities, depending on high culture for their status and their livings. For them, literature, like the universities themselves, appeared the aesthetic arm of capitalist ideology, a cultural instrument of a corrupt and repressive social order. The "authoritarian" old literature was equated with a police state, and distinguished critics like Meyer Abrams, Walter Jackson Bate, and the younger E. D. Hirsch, who continued to insist that a work of literature had a specific meaning locked in place in its own language, were spoken of as "class police" who repressed free interpretation with "the night-stick of verification and the handcuffs of validity." The "idea that the Truth is One— unambiguous, self-consistent, and knowable," which was certainly a central tenet of the old humanistic literature, as it has been indeed at of all traditional theories of knowledge, was denounced by a radical critic as one of "the murderous fictions of our history." Another critic, remembering a remark by Lenin on music, said that "good writing is counterrevolutionary."

Ours is a strange time, but it has in it, as the words quoted above suggest, few things stranger than the violence and even hatred with which the old literature was deconstructed by those who earn their living teaching and writing about it. They stood in line, fought for a place at the front of it, to demonstrate the meanness and emptiness of books and poems that had long been read and taught as the highest achievements of the human spirit. Humanism became a term of contempt, and the work of literature an illusion. The attack has abated, the old literature being stone dead, but at the moment, in 1990, the most popular subjects of criticism and undergraduate and graduate courses are still those that demonstrate how meaningless, or paradoxically, how wicked and antiprogressive, the old literature has been, how meaningless is its language, how badly it has treated those who are not white, how regularly it has voiced an aristocratic jackbooted ethos or propagandized for a brutally materialistic capitalism. As David Brooks says, describing the way in which the literary curriculum at Duke was recast in the 1980s to embody the new politics and the hatred of the old literature: "Marx is stood on his head. Literature does not reflect material conditions; it creates them. Domination, imperialism, racism and sexism are caused by their depiction in the books championed by the white male elite."

The intensity and extent of the literary power struggle of recent years appear sharply when we look not at the views of single critics but at the total achievement of the critical revolution. The term *literature*, once used with confidence that it referred to an objective, well-defined group of writings of a specifically literary type—"the best that has been thought and said," the "spontaneous overflow of powerful feelings," "just representations of general nature"—disappeared with the application of a little analysis. Literature was soon shown to be a farrago made up of poetry and prose, fiction and fact, stories and plays and novels and poems and biographies and pieces of history and philosophy. Sacred texts mingle with court entertainments, and oral epics celebrating the bloody deeds of tribal heroes exist as literature alongside exquisitely refined memories, written in the privacy and silence of a cork-lined room, of the taste of a cookie in childhood. Attempts to identify some universal literary principle, most often either the psychological power of the imagination that was said to have generated all literary texts, or the concept of fictionality said to distinguish literature from all other forms of writing, soon trailed away in vagueness and lost their reality, not only in the indeterminacy of the concepts but among the endless variety of works that have historically been considered literary. Lyrics that express the direct feelings of the poet, biographical narratives, naturalistic novels, symbolic poems, confessions *de profundis* and all the other variety included in literature declare its undeniable synthetic nature. E. Donald Hirsch, usually a quite conservative critic, disintegrated literary essentialism and the canon that objectified it in a short, provocatively titled article, "What Isn't Literature." It did not take a very long argument or much evidence to show conclusively that people do not agree among themselves about which particular works constitute literature and that the canon is in constant change. When Hirsch finishes his short article, all the substance has leached out of the word *literature*, and it has become only verbal ectoplasm, referring, if to anything at all, only to the varying pieces of writing people have loosely thought at one time or another as falling under this heading.

Genres like tragedy and comedy, once a bastion of literary reality, have become as soft as the word *literature*. Style, form, and structure, too, have lost their substance under the cold eye of the deconstructing critic. Metaphor, image, symbol, irony, ambiguity, and all the many figures of speech that were once thought to distinguish literature from other modes of discourse are by now only tropes or rhetorical devices, sleights of language, as it were, used to create illusions of truth or reality. For all their earlier importance and seeming solidity, these concepts are now only smaller bodies dotted about the elephants' graveyard of literary history among the bigger carcasses of literature past, like the creative imagination, art for art's sake, beauty, and myth.

Deconstruction offered itself as a disinterested search for truth, a rigorous philosophical inquiry into such fundamental literary matters as writing and meaning that had hitherto been treated in the casual, even sloppy, fashion that showed up so painfully in the *Lady Chatterley* testimony. Rigorously logical it has been, but its program and its metaphors show it to have been from the beginning a new-left form of political action with a neo-Marxist conception of society as the scene of a relentless power struggle. The decision about what a text means, interpretation, has been portrayed, for example, as a battle in the class war, and literary iconoclasm as a crucial part of the struggle for democratic freedom. Roland Barthes, for example, found tyranny in a "classic criticism [which] has never paid any attention to the reader; for it, the writer is the only person in literature." Barthes and others have cast the reader or audience in the role of the oppressed proletariat, while the traditional writer and the classical work of literary art have become the cultural exploiters of the old social order, using their authority to control and limit meaning.

Extending the Marxist scheme, literary revolution took the form of empowering the literary sansculottes to decide what a text means by legitimating the interpretations of the reader, and at the same time overthrowing the exploitative owners of meaning, the old authoritarian concept of literature and the rentier authors. Various types of reader-response criticism and reception aesthetics showed readers that they were free to interpret in any way they saw fit texts which in themselves either had no meaning, or were deficient in meaning, or contained infinite possibilities of meaning. The heroic creators, always male, of great works of literature in the past—Aeschylus, Virgil, Dante, Shakespeare—were dispossessed of their literary property by being reduced to "scriptors" who did not create but merely exploited the stock of ideas common to their languages and times. Language now writes, not the author, in Heidegger's famous phrasing, and "texts," not works of art, are created not in the mind of the author but by language and culture, which collect in the mind and flow through the hand, as it were, of the scriptor, onto the page. The author, that central pillar of romantic and modern literature, whose creative imagination was once considered the validating source of all art, was finally sent to the guillotine. Michel Foucault, "What Is an Author?" and Roland Barthes, "The Death of the Author," insist that the "author" is only a historical idea, as Barthes says, "formulated by and appropriate to the social beliefs of democratic, capitalistic society with its emphasis on the individual."

Harold Bloom, a politically conservative but psychologically radical critic, salvaged a little, but only a little, dignity for the old romantic artist by making him, instead of a scriptor, a literary freedom fighter, an Oedipal terrorist, desperately trying to escape the shadow of his predecessor-fathers in order to write something new and authoritatively his own. Writing in this view is a power struggle between generations, with the latecomer condemned to an endless anxiety of influence, from which escape into the creation of something genuinely new and authentically personal comes only by error or lucky accident. In this grim view of the literary scene, the old generous concepts of influence and imitation in which one writer learned from and built on the poetic achievements of predecessors, creating, if not literary progress, then still continuity and historical development in literature, become only another of the myths the past constructed to allow human beings to think well of themselves. In its place Bloom offers "the anxiety of influence," a darkling struggle against fathers, in which the later poets are by necessity revolutionaries who must struggle desperately to create something new in the great shadows cast by their predecessors. Only "strong" Promethean writers, according to Bloom, find in themselves authentically original sounds and ideas rather than merely echoing the styles of earlier writers that have invaded and possessed the psyches and the writing of "weak" writers.

In the patriarchal past, criticism, too, though now the voice of freedom, was a repressive force, defending the authority of the text and the author by enforcing interpretative orthodoxy. Susan Sontag, speaking for many others in her famous essay, "Against Interpretation," rebelled against this heavy burden, "from now to the end of consciousness we are stuck with the task of defending art [which] poisons our sensibilities" by forcing them to exist in a "shadow world of the intellect." The endless criticism and body of interpretation that has accumulated offers only a "hypertrophy of the intellect," a "revenge of the intellect upon art" to make it "manageable" and "comfortable." Be done with it, and with critics, Sontag exhorts, and, criticism having withered away, let us move on to an "erotics of art" in which each is free to find any meaning in a text in a quest for personal satisfaction.

Others, themselves critics with a considerable investment in criticism, have not wanted to be so quick to be done with criticism, and have found a way to bring criticism into the revolutionary party by casting the critic in the familiar role of the intellectual committed to the class struggle and the cause of the proletariat, a Marx, Engels, Bakunin, Lenin. All readers are equal, of course, but the reader as critic is so equal that he or she assumes the authority once held by the monarchical writer in the literary hierarchy. "Let him be Caesar!" Geoffrey Hartman, in "Literary Commentary as Literature," tears down the traditional literary class structure that has made critics and criticism second-class citizens to poets and poetry, freeing critics from their "positive or reviewing function, from . . . subordination to the thing commented on." Instead, he offers a new type of creative criticism like that of Schlegel, Valéry, Ortega, Freud, and Heidegger, dialectic, ironic, concerned with transcendent ideas. Open and difficult, this new criticism will transcend poetry by being more "difficult" than poetry. Its "intellectual poems" will be *demonic*, a perpetual literary Maoism, always transvaluing and turning things, like the ranking of the poets, around, always recontextualizing, putting literary things, which are themselves not firm, in new settings and new arrangements. In reading this it is instructive to remember how recently T. S. Eliot in his essay "The Function of Criticism" was able to say without fear of contradiction that "no exponent of criticism . . . has, I presume, ever made the preposterous assumption that criticism is an autotelic activity."

The revolt of the critic-readers against the old literature required not only the death of authors, and their running dogs, the old-style critics, who controlled interpretation and terrorized readers, but the demolition of the authority of the monumental work of art as well, the "verbal icon" or "the well-wrought urn." Wimsatt foresaw and labeled this iconoclasm "battering the object," the object being the single, unique work of art, or even the conception of literature itself, so carefully isolated from its social context and idealized by romantic and modern critical theory "as a separately existent and in some sense autonomous or autotelic entity." Various modern types of literary study have disintegrated and redistributed the parts of such great literary monuments as *The Iliad, King Lear, The Brothers Karamazov* that had stood at the center of humanistic literature making permanent statements about absolute truths. Phenomenological and psychoanalytic criticism, for example, broke down the integrity of the single work of literary art in a search for the mind of the author, which was reconstituted by assembling the bits and pieces of the total oeuvre in new configurations. Reader-response or reception aesthetics drain the autonomous work of art of its meaning by relocating the meaning-making power to the eyes of the beholders, who no longer find meaning in *Hamlet* or *Faust* but supply it from their own understanding.

The assault on the literary masterpieces has been unrelenting, and when they have been allowed a meaning in their own right, that meaning has been discovered to be negative. A group of social criticisms—Marxism, new historicism, feminism, and certain kinds of psychoanalytic criticism—have totally discounted the moral integrity and the truthfulness of the literary text. These modes of literary interpretation have discounted literature by accusing it of ignorance at best, bad faith at worst, of playing a purposeful and cunning part in the imperialistic and financial power games of Western society, imposing and strengthening the hegemony of one class, or sex, or ideology, or race over others. In these views, literature, not long ago considered to be the most authentic language of humanity, expressing its highest abilities and aspirations, diminishes to propaganda, its structure or form to the rhetoric of persuasion, and its values to ideology. The discrediting of the old masterpieces of literature is summed up in their transition from "works" to "texts," the latter being any socially constructed belief, a book, an institution, a language, a concept, even, like "the Renaissance."

The Bastilles of the old literature, the reality of "literature," the creativity of the author, the superiority of authors and literary works to critics and readers, and the integrity of the literary art work, have now all been stormed. The attackers carried many banners, but all were associated with the political radicalism of recent decades, and all drew their authority in varying ways and degrees from two closely connected skepticisms, structuralism and post-structuralism or deconstruction, which were the enabling philosophies of the new left. Applied to literature, these philosophies placed literature in a setting totally different from the scene created for it by humanism.

In the structuralist world, humanism's creative individual, represented in literature by the imaginative artist, disappears. Life and world are transformed into an endless series of interlocking games. Each game set contains an arbitrary number of pieces, but they are the only pieces that matter—everything else is "noise"—and they can be moved only in accordance with fixed and invariable rules of combination. These social games, of which language is the model, and art and literature central instances, are nonreferential in that they do not reflect any prior natural reality. From the structuralist viewpoint, a literary text is not mimetic, a representation, even an indirect representation, of something outside itself like the fall of Troy or the growth of a poet's mind, but one instance of a literary game, combining a chosen number of "literary" themes in some acceptable variant of the "literary" manner. Nor is literature historical (diachronic) in the sense that its meaning, say, for example, the evolution of consciousness, is established by developments in a succession of literary works over time. Its reality, instead, is that of the moment and the relationship (synchronic) at that point in time of all the parts of the literary system. *Hamlet,* for example, is not to be understood in the context of England in 1600, or in the long line of Western tragedies beginning with the Greeks, or in terms of what it may seem to say about such "universal" themes as the helplessness of thought in the face of political power. In the structuralist paradigm, its meaning is instead to be derived from its place in the contemporary literary set, either then or now, what things it is like, other revenge tragedies, what things it is unlike, comedies.

Individuals create nothing but simply take the pieces their culture offers them and combine and recombine them by the rules of the particular cultural game they are playing. Literature as a part of culture is, like culture itself, only one of the human meaning games, along with an infinity of other games, played out continuously in front of a meaningless and incoherent universe to produce what passes as meaning and truth. No two literary games—oral poetry, Horatian satire, *The Faerie Queene*, or the novels of Dickens—are ever the same, thus the endless variety. The rules, such as binary opposition, or metaphorical substitution of equivalent terms, always provide for an orderly arrangement of the parts, thus producing a meaning based on nothing more substantial than similarities and differences of the parts to one another. In this structuralist perspective, humanistic literature, which had presented itself as the written expression in a powerful style of deep truths discovered and elaborated over time by remarkable individuals, no longer made sense. Literature could only be literary games played out with a number of basic set pieces, standardized mythemes, a repertory of type characters, a rhetoric of tropes, a taxonomy of genres, Propp's basic plots. These elements can be and have been endlessly combined and rearranged to create the cultural game of literature. Polonius's genre theory, "tragedy, comedy, history, pastoral, pastoral-comical, historical-pastoral, tragical-historical, tragical-comical-historical-pastoral," is no longer so ridiculous as it once was.

Culture in the structuralist view is a set of games with arbitrary pieces, governed by provisional rules, giving artificial meaning to human activity, played out in front of a meaningless nature and a pointless past. But where structuralism had tended to privilege the system, as in Saussure's *la langue* or the binary oppositions of Lévi-Strauss's structuralist anthropology, as an innate or at least a logical way of constructing meaning, deconstruction or post-structuralism looked with deep skepticism at the structuralist meaning-making machinery. Super-close readings of the language of literary texts revealed that all concepts and the words representing them rested ultimately on nothing. The reality established in writing by various structural devices such as traces of system, binary opposition, or difference of one element to another—sign and signified, culture and nature, the raw and the cooked—are always found on close examination to be incomplete and contradictory illusions. Meaning is established by reference to central terms—God or nature or goodness—but each of these terms in turn is dependent on the meaning of its successor, whose validity in turn can be established only by its successor. Discourse is thus an endless deferral of reality, an infinite regress, leading ultimately to the abyss of nothing and nowhere. All words and texts are indeterminate, carrying opposing, contradictory significations, which can be teased out of language to reveal its uncontrollable multiplicity of meanings, so numerous that they in the end cancel out, leaving writer and reader facing the void where presence gives way to infinite absence. All human "discourse" tries to make meaning not inside a mystery behind which invisible truths are concealed, but within an emptiness which cannot support the dreams of meaning. In the view of deconstruction, literature, either the single text or the total institution, provides a particularly revealing model of human efforts to construct a meaningful reality with words, and of the inability of doing so in any final and absolute form.

It already requires an effort to remember that it is not an unalterable fact that language *is* radically indeterminate, or that the author *is* dead, or that there *is* no such thing as literature. Terry Eagleton can state flatly, without fear of contradiction, that "literature is an ideology" and one of the means "by which certain social groups exercise and maintain power over others," and most literary people nod their heads in sage agreement. It takes an enormous effort to remember, as if the old texts and the old beliefs had already gone down some Orwellian "memory hole," that Virginia Woolf in an admired essay printed in 1924, "Mr. Bennett and Mrs. Brown," made with complete plausibility and faultless logic exactly the opposite case. True literature, she said, like "*Tristram Shandy* or *Pride and Prejudice* is complete in itself; it is self-contained; it leaves one with no desire to do anything, except indeed to read the book again, and to understand it better. . . . Sterne and Jane Austen were interested in things in themselves; character in itself; in the book in itself. Therefore everything was inside the book, nothing outside."

Older humanistic views like Woolf's about the integrity of the literary work and its ineradicable meaning, about the creative imagination of the authors of literature and the perfection of the created artifact, about the great tradition of literary masterpieces and the long line of imitation and influence, all beliefs which were alive and intellectually potent only yesterday, have disappeared as completely as if they had been vaporized. Now, with equal plausibility and equally well marshaled facts, everyone seems to agree that there are no works of art, only texts open to endless interpretation, that the authors have disappeared into a sea of intertextuality, that all writing is a part of the struggle for power to control interpretation, that the great writer violently rejects all predecessors, that literature has no essence, and that writing is endlessly indeterminate, finally empty of meaning, or, what comes to the same thing, overflowing with an excess of meanings. Deconstruction swept literature before it, and even if its moment too is passing, as seems the case, it has rearranged the literary world, though not much else, so completely as to make it unlikely that there will ever be a return to the humanistic and positivistic assumptions that once supported romantic and modernist literature.

The deconstruction of the old humanistic order of literature regularly presented itself, in spite of its revolutionary rhetoric and its radical political connections, as nothing anyone need be much alarmed by.

Paul De Man regularly said that he was only reading the literary text with all the exactitude that older precise ways of reading the literary text, such as new criticism or formalism, had proposed in theory but never entirely achieved in practice. This, despite a certain plausibility, was not the case, of course. The razor-close readings of deconstruction always eventuate in discovering that all texts, because of the indeterminate nature of language, contradict themselves in ways that cancel out even the possibility of any meaning, however ironic or ambiguous, and this is about as far away as it is possible to get from the position of the new criticism that works of literature are sacred texts so intensely meaningful that any paraphrase is heresy. Jacques Derrida and J. Hillis Miller, along with Jonathan Culler and other notorious deconstructors, regularly deny the nihilistic tendencies of deconstruction, insisting that they do not so much deny the possibility of meaning in language as they free readers from the burdens of imposed and illusory single meanings to make possible a variety of meanings suiting human needs. In this, as in much else, they follow Nietzsche, who spoke of a "gay science," a "happy and dextrous negotiation of a surplus, or excess of meaning."

They follow Nietzsche in other ways as well, for deconstruction is a latter-day application of an intellectual and social relativism that has been undermining positivism in Western culture throughout the twentieth century. The project of this broad and powerful current of thought, as Brian Rotman sums it up, "is one of unmasking. What it has to show is how the whole apparatus of reason built on logic is nothing but a vast system of persuasion: logic is rhetoric, truth an illusion produced by argument; and all difference such as essence/appearance, rational/irrational, true/false and so on, lacking any grounding in an absolute outside themselves, have no more authority than the language and culture producing them." From scientific theories of relativity, uncertainty and probability, through cultural anthropology and history of ideas, to existentialism and structural linguistics, Western thinkers have increasingly pictured a cosmos where reality and truth stand on nothing except the bias of the observer.

Seen in the context of the history of ideas, it is not so surprising that deconstruction brought these views to bear on literature, as that it took so long for them to reach that institution. The old literature with its quaint beliefs in creative geniuses, iconic works of art, myths, and eternal meanings survived surprisingly long. What is remarkable and calls for explanation is the speed and the thoroughness with which the deconstructive argument swept the literary world, and this brings us back to a consideration of the social circumstances in which "the triumph of theory" occurred. The remaking of literature may have been in some large sense historically inevitable, but the immediate energy that drove it forward was classically Marxist, a class struggle within the literary institution for the means of intellectual production. Deconstruction always offered itself as purely philosophical in the grand sense of seeking truth, no matter how disillusioning, and idealistically political in the broad sense of furthering the universal causes of freedom and equality. It cannot be ignored, however, that the critical revolution of recent years has ended with the academic critics almost totally in control of literature, the goal they have long sought. Not only have they removed it physically from the outer world to within the walls of the academy, but they have demystified and annihilated the old literary system of romanticism and modernism ruled over by great authors and literary masterworks, in which criticism was only a humble servant. Structuralism and deconstruction are criticism-oriented theories. Philosophically difficult, abstract and endlessly complex, they are the work of experts and require explanation by experts. The layman who handles them is like Brer Rabbit trying to deal with the Tar Baby. They are theoretical systems that give central importance to systems such as *la langue* in the making of literature and meaning. And finally, since they authorize an infinity of interpretations, they provide an endless protected marketplace for the critics who trade in interpretation.

The institutional power struggle was legitimated, masked really, and further energized by the democratic social revolution and the turbulence that came to the universities of the 1960s, in which Trilling rightly saw the death of humanistic literature, partly at least by its own hand. In the setting of the larger revolution, criticism's literary power grab appeared only another reach for freedom and escape from an irrational authority. Legitimated by deconstruction, the revolution has continued to express itself in the 1970s and 1980s inside the departments of literature as a variety of aggressive social causes such as feminism, racial tolerance, moral relativism, ethnicity, and sexual freedom, all rejecting traditional forms of authority, intellectual and social, and demanding that literature be used to further their own social and political programs.

against ethical lapse [handwritten marginal note]

The militancy of deconstruction and the radical social movements that have accompanied it was encouraged by the appearance in the 1970s of a new proletariat of disappointed literary academics. Deconstruction has been largely the creation of sophisticated mandarins teaching in the more prestigious universities, but their audience has been in large part a group of marginal young academics, including a large number, a majority even, of women, and members of various minorities who wanted to break into what had previously been a preserve of white, usually Protestant, males. A number of circumstances turned this new generation of teacher-scholars into an intellectual proletariat and radicalized them.

Although the colleges and universities were still expanding, hard times came to literature in the 1970s and 1980s as enrollments in literary courses dropped, reading and writing skills fell sharply, and the brighter students began to go to law and medical school rather than to the graduate schools of arts and sciences. Looking back in a report of September 12, 1988, Lynne V. Cheney, head of the National Endowment for the Humanities, reported that over the past two decades while the number of bachelor's degrees given overall was increasing by 88 percent, degrees in the humanities were decreasing by 33 percent. History lost the most, 43 percent, but philosophy went down by 35 percent, English by 33 percent, and foreign languages by 29 percent. These figures have been attacked by those in whose interest it is to insist that nothing has really happened in recent years and that all is well, perhaps even improving, with literature and the humanities; but however the count is conducted it shows a precipitous drop in the study of these subjects. Government supported National Defense Education Act and foundation fellowships for graduate study in the humanities brought into being by Sputnik disappeared during this time, and the general shrinkage of the job market drove students toward subjects that could help them get a job on graduation. By 1975, conservative estimates, based on the ratio of advertised jobs to Ph.D.s granted, showed that there were at least six applicants for every teaching job. Taking economic advantage of the situation, and financially pressed themselves, university administrations began to marginalize the appointments in literature and other humanities by making more and more of them temporary, part-time, on the hourly pay scale but off the tenure track, and bare of benefits.

Amid this reduction of what had been a profession to a minimal kind of job, the country became acutely aware that its young people could no longer read or write at the levels established as the norm by previous generations. The reasons for the situation are complex, as we shall see when we look at the "literacy crisis." It resulted partly from falling literacy standards in the public schools, partly from the increased use of television, and partly from the attempt to educate large numbers of ill-prepared students from social groups that previously had not gone to school. Whatever the causes and their complexity, talk of a crisis spread widely, and a national drive was launched to teach college students how to write. The work was assigned inevitably to English departments, and the teaching of English in this country became what it still largely remains, outside a few privileged universities and colleges, the teaching of writing rather than the Arnoldian mission of teaching the great works of literature to make reason and the will of God prevail. In the 1970s and 1980s large numbers of intelligent, highly educated young people who had expected to become scholars and professors of literature at distinguished universities slipped back down the social scale to being poorly paid writing masters at marginal colleges with minimal admission and retention standards.

These were for a time the only jobs available, and those who filled them could not but feel betrayed by the establishment that had recruited and trained them. They seemed unfairly frozen out of the scholarly world they had expected to be welcomed into, and the disappointment radicalized them. For them it looked not like a treason of the clerks so much as a *trahison des maîtres*. Rejected and ignored by the old literary establishment, they naturally applauded and delighted in the critical iconoclasm that ripped the guts out of the old literature, and eagerly welcomed the new professional democracy that leveled all critics and made all interpretations equal. There is no doubt about what happened, and about the fact that it changed the teaching profession in literature around, but, except for cries of protest here and there in letters to editors, the situation has been almost ignored.

The result has been the radical politicization of literature, both criticism and teaching. In those classrooms where deconstructive theory prevails, literature is being taught as a type of intellectual Maoism, *the* revolutionary subject, in which the texts—and anything to hand is a text—are used to demonstrate the absurdity of any absolute truth and the duplicity of any attempt to pretend that there is or can be one. Students are sensitized to the relativism of all truth and encouraged to exercise an anarchic freedom to construct whatever kinds of truths are most attractive and useful. For others with more explicit political programs, literature has become a more overt move in the game of political and social power. Feminists, for example, most frequently teach literature as one of the tactics by which the patriarchy established and maintained male hegemony over the female, for example, *King Lear*, "Her voice was ever soft, gentle and low, an excellent thing in woman." Black studies and Third World studies, working on the assumption that inclusion in the literary canon confers cultural, and thence political, prestige, teach on social rather than aesthetic grounds. The traditional canon, largely the work of white, Western men, is examined for its support of imperialism and racism. Writings by blacks and authors of various ethnic origins, not previously considered significant enough to be included in the official literary canon, become the substance of courses in Black Literature, Women's Literature, and, by way of one example, Literature by Italian-Americans. Jane Tompkins has legitimated this extra-canonical literature by arguing that texts should be considered literature not on an aesthetic basis but solely on the grounds of the social influence they have had. *Uncle Tom's Cabin* by this standard becomes the great American novel of the nineteenth century.

Various types of Marxist criticism, the new historicism associated with Stephen Greenblatt, more dogmatic versions of Marxism in the writings of critics like Terry Eagleton and Fredric Jameson, followers of Foucault like Jonathan Arac, extend, in complicated modern ways, the old view that literature is determined by the primary means of production, technological and intellectual, and is necessarily an instrument in the class struggle for political control. Literature in these views is an instrument of power politics, almost always in the employ, directly or indirectly, of the establishment, so that teaching them becomes a consciousness-raising exposure of right-wing propaganda.

Texts have become primarily political documents, and seemingly gone forever is what Terry Eagleton (1989) has called "the poetic, or more generally the aesthetic, [which] has furnished English culture with one of its stoutest ideological shields against the barbarism of the ideological." Eagleton sums up in a hostile but accurate manner the old values of romantic and modern literature that were alive as recently as when Lionel Trilling looked out his window and saw the students blocking the entrance to Low Library as: "the dogmatic intuitionism of the imagination; the priority of local affections and unarguable allegiances; tradition as a spontaneous growth impervious to rational critique; the supposedly uncontrovertible nature of 'immediate' experience; the unquestionable superiority of the felt to the reasoned."

4

Literature and the Law:

The Moral Rights

of Artists

Art and literature, even today as in the past, often picture themselves outside and above the day-to-day world, in some removed imaginative setting, some intellectual equivalent of pastoral, or the kingdoms of faerie, not in the marketplace and the courtroom rubbing shoulders with greed, vanity, sex, money, and power. But art has always existed in and been at least partly defined by its place and function in the social world of the palace, the great house, the church, the universities, the legislature and law courts.

Never has the law been so active in artistic and literary affairs as at the present. "Jurists have become the most authoritative new students of literary motif and definers of genre," says one acute observer of literature in the courts, Neil Harris. The genre of satire has been particularly subject to definition by the courts because writings which might otherwise be actionable can 'scape whipping if it can be successfully argued that they are satire, and therefore a type of art privileged in its hostility. Usually the artistic claim is coupled with freedom of speech, so that aesthetics and the First Amendment regularly appear together. I discovered this

88

some years ago when, having earlier published some studies of satire, I was asked to testify as an expert witness that some songs that were only slightly modified copies of extremely popular musical pieces from a famous television children's program were in fact satire. The defense was to be that the intention of copying them had been to mock the originals in the manner of satire, not to capitalize on their popularity. Fortunately for me this case never came to court, for I did not look forward to a clever attorney asking questions that literary people have never settled, such as "What exactly is satire?" and "What are the distinguishing characteristics that allow you to say precisely and factually that this work is satire, while that is not?" and "How do you distinguish irony from satire? or comedy?"

While this case never came to court, a different case involving satire did, the 1987 Supreme Court case of *Hustler* v. Falwell. *Hustler*, a hard-core and pugnacious sex mag, is owned and edited by Larry Flynt, who earlier had been shot and crippled by a man who considered him and his explicit pictures of sex a danger to American society and a stench in the nostrils of the Lord. Condemned to spend his life in a wheelchair, Flynt later conceived a violent dislike for the evangelical TV gospeler, Jerry Falwell, who was portrayed in *Hustler* as both drunken and incestuous, with his mother in an outhouse, no less. When Falwell went to law, *Hustler* admitted the utter vulgarity and total falsity of what it had printed, but in addition to asserting First Amendment rights of free speech, contended that the attack was a type of satire, parody, that by its nature exaggerated in order to target effectively whatever it attacked. Everyone understood that what was said in a satire was not to be taken for literal truth but as licensed artistic overstatement. The court decided in favor of *Hustler* and against Falwell, and thereby, without being aware of the questions of literary theory involved, pronounced on a long and heated literary issue, "Does satire really harm its targets?" No question in satire has been more fiercely debated, usually taking the form of the satirist declaring that he attacks the vice, not the person, and that no one whose conscience is clear need fear the whip. If cornered by victims unpersuaded by these arguments, the satirist has traditionally added that words can't really harm anyone, or that it was only in good fun, or if pressed really hard, that the concealed moral ugliness of the vice attacked required violent and obscene language to expose it for what it truly was. When his interlocutor in *The Epilogue to the Satires, Dialogue II*, objects to a particularly unpleasant piece of satiric language—

> This filthy Simile, this beastly Line,
> Quite turns my stomach

Alexander Pope defends himself in terms that Larry Flynt could have used had he known them, and the Supreme Court of the United States would have accepted as valid legal reasoning:

> So does Flatt'ry mine;
> And all your Courtly Civet-Cats can vent,
> Perfume to you, to me is Excrement.

In our litigious and avaricious times, artistic questions of many kinds have found their way more and more often into legal proceedings, and each time they do, the courts or quasi-legal bodies have given artistic values the reality of law. The *New York Times* (October 21, 1986), for example, reported that Bess Myerson (once Miss America and now a convicted shoplifter recently tried and found not guilty of bribing a judge to lower her lover's alimony) had been as commissioner of culture in New York City certifying people as artists. The real value of such certification was considerable, for it entitled those officially stamped as artists to subsidized city housing in special blocks of apartments and to exemption from restrictions limiting conversion of desirable loft space to studios. Certification was also said to help in getting grants from government agencies and private foundations, anxious to be assured, presumably, that they were giving their money to true artists and not to impostors. Commissioner Myerson used typical bureaucratic standards, such as the number of shows, previous grants and fellowships, amounts published and by whom, reviews, and so forth to decide who was and who was not a true artist. But the result was to legitimate, in a very substantial way, the ancient claim of the romantic artist to being a superior person worthy of special treatment by society, such as housing subsidies and exemptions from laws applying to ordinary folk.

The United States Supreme Court, by way of another example of the way law has recently been legitimating romantic art theory, in April 1987 upheld a federal statute "classifying as 'political propaganda' all foreign government films that might influence public opinion on United States foreign policies." The Court thus stigmatized as propaganda, though it did not prohibit the showing of three Canadian films dealing with nuclear war and acid rain. Although the opinion suggested that "propaganda" might be considered a neutral term, the decision legalized the distinction that romantic aesthetics has long made between authentic art, which is nonutilitarian and without intent to persuade ("a poem should not mean but be"), and propaganda, a type of false art that seeks to persuade people to think and act in certain ways. Virginia Woolf, again in "Mr. Bennett and Mrs. Brown," wondered whether this kind of sub-art that tries to do something should be called art at all since it leaves "one with so strange a feeling of incompleteness and dissatisfaction. In order to complete [it] it seems necessary to do something—to join a society, or more desperately, to write a cheque."

About a hundred city, state, and county governments have recently enacted "percent for art" programs, requiring that 1 percent of the construction costs for new public buildings be spent on art, such as statues, murals, fountains, and other works with aesthetic value. The requirement at first caused little controversy, but the amounts became larger and larger as construction costs rose. The builders of gambling casinos in Atlantic City, who fell under the statute as a result of being regulated by the state of New Jersey, balked at the requirement that they spend large amounts on elaborate chandeliers and freeform art. The Connecticut legislature in 1989, in a time of financial difficulty, found itself spending several hundred thousand dollars for art in the new prisons it was building. Questions then arose as to whether prisons needed art, whether the prisoners deserved it, and even if they did whether it improved them in any significant way. When the "percent for art" laws were designed and passed they were intended as only straightforward support for art, taking for granted the romantic assumption that art is a definite kind of thing that can be distinguished from non-art without any kind of metaphysical difficulties and that it is so positive a force in the world that it should be considered a human "right," not to be denied to anyone, even prisoners. No one dreamed that they would end up in such quandaries as that in which a supporter of art for prisons in the Connecticut legislature found himself: "The real issue is how do you make the distinction between people who deserve this kind of quality in their environment and those who don't. . . . Will this lead us to believe that people who are emotionally or mentally disturbed don't deserve it either" (*New York Times*, March 25, 1989). In a way that would have amused the great romantic troublemakers like Shelley and Hugo, another official saw art as an irenic force: "There is a direct correlation between the harshness of a prison setting and the level of violence. Whatever we can do to make [prison] safer [by putting art in it] is owed to those people" (Kirk Johnson).

Coleridge pronounced the artist's creative imagination, "the prime agent of all human perception, and . . . a repetition in the finite mind of the eternal act of creation in the infinite I AM," and the courts continue to accept, almost without question, that the special nature of the artists' creative power gives them rights in their work unknown in other kinds of property. As the distinguished legal historian of copyright Lord Goodman says, "the whole of the modern extensions of copyright seeks to improve the rights of [the] artistic creator rather than to diminish them." International copyright agreements in 1892 made those rights worldwide, and the latest U.S. copyright act of 1978 extended, as in Britain, copyright to the life of the author plus fifty years. In 1989 the Supreme Court further strengthened the hands of the writers and painters in the ongoing battle over intellectual property by ruling that even when artistic work is done by freelance artists under contract, an article or a magazine cover, for example, the business paying for the work has only bought the rights to use the work once. Any republication or adaptation rights belong to the creator. A federal circuit court in the same year found that a legal technicality allowed Janet Malcolm writing for the *New Yorker* to escape being liable for attributing to Geoffrey Masson as direct quotations remarks he had never made about the Freud archives.

Limits on authors' rights under the law are few. The vaguely defined doctrine of "fair use" allows reviewers and scholars to quote without payment limited numbers of words, and there is a trifling requirement that copies of a printed work be deposited without payment in a few designated copyright libraries, but overwhelmingly the law favors the artist. Even unpublished work like letters belongs to the author for life plus fifty years — only the physical paper on which the letter or manuscript is written belongs to the recipient or legal possessor of the unpublished material. Just how far the courts are willing to go in considering both the author and his writing specially privileged became evident when J. D. Salinger, an author who fetishizes privacy, blocked the publication of a biography of himself, written by Ian Hamilton, by legally preventing the use not only of excerpts from his unpublished letters but even paraphrases of the contents of those letters. The biography was eventually published in 1988 by Random House, which had a sizable advance tied up in the work, but it was much shorter than its original length and the tone was one of considerable exasperation toward Salinger.

Perhaps the only outstanding exceptions in law to the romantic primacy of the artist are the various "Son-of-Sam" laws, designed to prevent convicted criminals from profiting from their crime. The name comes from a sensational case of a serial killer who ambushed and shot a number of young couples making love in isolated places. When apprehended, the killer, David Berkowitz, said that he had been ordered to kill by a dog that belonged to Sam Carr, a neighbor. Later when some enterprising "as told to" writers and a publisher tried to capitalize on a confessional book about the crimes, the Son-of-Sam law, the first of many, was hastily passed in New York State requiring that any payment the criminal receives for works describing his or her crime must be given to the victims or their heirs, or to victims of other crimes. A sum of $118,000 from movie and book deals was later given to eight Son-of-Sam victims or their families in New York.

So sacred is the author's relationship to his or her work, however, that even in Son-of-Sam cases anxious authors and selfless publishers have felt that they have a chance of successfully challenging the law. Some years ago, Jean Harris, headmistress of the fashionable Madeira School in Washington, D.C., emptied her pistol into the lover who had discarded her, the famous "Scarsdale Diet Doc," who had made a fortune advising people on less violent ways to lose weight. After some years in jail, during which she wrote her memoirs, including, of course, descriptions of the crime and the trial, she petitioned the board set up to handle Son-of-Sam cases to allow her to receive the royalties from her book. The profits were to be used, she said, to improve the lives of the young women incarcerated with her. She was turned down, however, and the money went to the heirs of her victim.

But publishers and authors never despair in their quest for justice, and in August 1987, Simon & Schuster, planning to publish a book about the life of a career criminal, written with his help, brought suit against the New York State Crime Board, claiming that the Son-of-Sam law had a chilling effect on First Amendment free-speech rights.

These laws would in the past have, it was asserted, prevented publishers from commissioning and printing great works of literature like Thoreau's "Civil Disobedience" or Martin Luther King's "Letter from Birmingham Jail." Strangely unmentioned were famous writers like Jean Genet, who, after a life as a thief, got his real start as a writer in jail, or Dostoyevski, whose art flourished while he was incarcerated.

At the very moment that its plausibility is waning in the larger world, the ideology of romantic and modern art, especially visual art, seems to have found a last refuge in the most conservative of institutions, the law, and in liberal politics, where the defense of the arts also still plays well. The major push literally to legitimate the privileged nature of art and the artist has taken the form of a group of laws designed to define and establish the so-called moral rights of artists. With the Massachusetts legislature leading the way, as it often does in artistic matters, many states already have passed laws prohibiting any changes in a work of art by its legal owner unless the change is agreed to by the artist who made it. Since money and property rights are the major issues, it is as difficult to see where *moral* rights are involved as it is to understand why a sales tax that adds only tax to a product should be called a "*value*-added tax." But political language grows increasingly inspired, and a national moral-rights bill was introduced in the Congress in 1987 and subsequent years by Senator Edward Kennedy. This proposed law has encountered considerable resistance because it not only prohibits any changes in a work of art without the consent of the artist but protects an even higher moral right, requiring that the artist get 7 percent of any appreciation of value when the work is resold, if the original cost was over $1,000 and the appreciation more than 150 percent. It is important to realize just how much money is at stake along with the morality. It was reported in 1989 that about $600 million was spent at art auctions in New York City during the first two weeks in May. Modern works as well as classics were commanding high prices, $11.5 million for a

Jackson Pollock, *No. 8, 1950.* An Andy Warhol, *Shot Red Marilyn,* a forty-inch square pop picture of Marilyn Monroe, was sold for $4.07 million. A nickel-plated copper wire wastebasket by Emile-Jacques Ruhlmann went for a mere $33,000, but an Egon Schiele, bought and sold three times in four years, was going for $3.5 million. The dead fetch the most, Van Gogh a record $53.9 million for *Irises* in 1987, and a Picasso self-portrait $47.9 million in 1989.

What can happen in the courts when the artist asserts his moral rights appears in the epic struggle of the sculptor Richard Serra, who sued the federal government to prevent what he called the "malicious" removal of his work *Tilted Arc,* a 12-foot-high, 112-foot-long steel wall, from the plaza near the Jacob Javits Federal Building in New York. Serra works on the heroic scale, and moving his work involves more than aesthetics. One of his pieces—shades of the commander and Don Giovanni!—killed a worker in Minneapolis in the early 1970s when it was being moved, while a sixteen-ton oeuvre, measuring 17 by 14 feet, toppled off the jacks in a So-Ho gallery in October 1988, pinning two men to the floor, knocking down several supports in the building, causing several walls to crack, floors to sag, and a standpipe to break, and flooding the building.

When, according to the *New York Times* (October 27, 1988), "more than 1,000 Government employees . . . signed a petition asking that the curved wall of three rusted steel plates [of *Tilted Arc*] be removed because it blocks access to the building, disrupts traffic patterns and 'destroys the plaza's vistas and amenities,'" Serra responded that "his work is [so] integral to the space and the space to the work [that] the two cannot be divorced without defacing the sculpture." Any change in location of his "site-specific" work, he insisted, would violate his First Amendment right to free speech, his Fifth Amendment right to due process, as well as his moral rights as an artist. In March 1989, after the federal circuit court had refused to issue an injunction, *Tilted Arc* was at last removed to a government motor compound in Brooklyn.

There was one last effort to stop the removal when Congress after many years' delay agreed to the United States becoming a signatory to the International Copyright Agreement, which contains a modified rights of artists clause. But the protection seemed unlikely to hold in American courts, and *Tilted Arc* was trucked ignominiously away, followed by the disillusioned cries of the hapless artist, bitter to the last, "This Government is savage, it is eating its culture. I don't think this country has ever destroyed a major work of art before."

The moral right of another artist came up in 1984 in a different way, though it didn't get to court, when the playwright Samuel Beckett, represented by his publisher, Barney Rosset, protested a production change by Robert Brustein, of the setting in his play *Endgame* to a subway station, with black actors playing the father and son. After being denounced as a racist by Actors' Equity, Rosset complained that "All I'm saying is that taking all the factors together—that the father and son were black and the mother was white—added a dimension to the play Beckett had not put there."

Moral rights have come up in a much more heated way in connection with recent transformations, made possible by computer technology, of old black-and-white films to color. The changes are being made by Ted Turner, the legal owner of the films, for showing on his television network to large numbers of viewers who prefer color to black and white. When he was accused of "desecrations" of the masterpieces of film art, his response sounded like a combination of John Locke and the Republican National Committee on property: "The last time I looked, I owned them!" But the film, the most recent of the arts, already has acquired a mythology, and directors and actors like James Stewart and the late John Huston protested violently that the coloring of films like *The Maltese Falcon* and *Mr. Deeds Goes to Washington* was nothing less than an irremediable sacrilege. Since the black-and-white prints remained, even while there were colored copies, it is not clear how the films were changed or harmed, but Congress held hearings on the matter, and Woody Allen among other stars appeared to testify about film being the modern art and the inalienable possession of the artists, actors and directors who made it. Cameramen, scriptwriters, and cutters were apparently insufficiently creative to be worthy of mention.

In Britain, in another extension of moral rights, royalties are now paid each time a book is taken from one of a number of trial libraries, just as payments are made on music each time a piece still under copyright is played. "Posthumous copyright" is still another proposed "moral right" which would distribute the royalties of dead writers among living writers rather than to the legal heirs, presumably on the theory that since writing is a sacred calling, the rights of any author, living or dead, take precedence always over those of anyone who is not a writer.

It is not just the artist but his or her work as well that is presently being legally privileged beyond the wildest dreams of the earlier romantics. The recent words of two proponents of the moral rights of artists legislation, Schuyler Chapin and Alberta Arthurs, reveal the way that high-romantic idealizations of the work of art can be used to lobby for legislation that accords special treatment to artistic things. "Art—physical, tangible, visual art—is more than a piece of property that some one or some institution owns. . . . In some real way [art works] belong to no one because they belong to all of us. They are among the most salient examples of the breadth and depth and complexity of human nature. Throughout time, our species has used the arts—this richer set of symbols that only humans have devised—to transmit the heritage of people and to express most profoundly their deepest human joys, sorrows and intuitions."

This self-stroking and clichéd conception of the art work as a sacred object testifying to "the breadth and depth and complexity of human nature" has been steadily gaining ground in the law in recent years. The recent claims made in connection with a new edition of the works of D. H. Lawrence would seem to take the privileges of art something near the limit. The details have been gathered by Michael Holroyd and Sandra Jobson in a splendid *TLS* article from which many of the following quotations about the matter are derived. Lawrence having died in 1929, his books had all emerged from the protection of copyright (life plus fifty years) in Britain by the beginning of 1981; and in the United States they entered the public domain at varying times based on the date of original copyright plus seventy-five years for all works copyrighted before 1978. Anyone who wished could presumably print them in Britain after 1981, and at some time later in the United States, without payments to the literary estate or the heirs.

At about this time, however, various Lawrence scholars, the Lawrence estate literary agent, and Cambridge University Press decided to produce a newly edited "authoritative" forty-volume edition of Lawrence's writings. When the first several volumes of the new edition appeared they contained a claim in the prefatory matter that the new edition constituted a basis for an entirely new copyright, running presumably for another fifty years: "Permission to reproduce this text entire or in part, or to quote from it, can be granted only by the Literary Executor of the Estate, Laurence Pollinger Ltd." The changes from previously published texts in the new editions were relatively slight in most cases, often only a few words or a bit of punctuation, but they were claimed to have established new rights not only over the passages changed, and only as changed, but over the entire text, even, it was implied, the parts that were identical with those of earlier manuscript and printed versions.

The editorial changes, it was being claimed, had, as it were, magically reconstituted the entire text and transformed it in its entirety, and in all its earlier forms, into a unique entity that could be copyrighted for another fifty years. Michael Black, the Cambridge editor for the new edition, disingenuously added that the Cambridge Lawrence was an "interesting departure from the normal run of scholarly editions in that it is indissolubly linked with the copyright of the main works themselves." Some indignation was expressed at this kind of humbug—indissolubly!—and Black, speaking for Cambridge Press, later retreated somewhat, though reluctantly, from the original position, allowing that "in many places in many texts the old version will either stand or be accepted by many people as good enough for working purposes, and I do not myself feel that Cambridge can realistically attempt to restrict the use of this material because it cannot demonstrate that distinctive features of the Cambridge edition are involved." "Good enough for working purposes" pretty well settles the matter along British class lines in regard to what really counts, but at least Cambridge University Press was no longer claiming the rights to the older forms of the text. There was still, however, a sophistic claim that *all* of the new text now belonged to them, the parts changed and the parts not changed, while only the old texts could be reprinted without permission. The logic of this is very contorted, since the unchanged portions of the new texts were identical with the same sections of the old text, but at least it saved face.

But though Cambridge may have retreated, the agent did not. "The Estate take a different view about this." In spite of the opinion of his copyright solicitor that only the changed parts could be considered copyrighted, and presumably only as changed, Pollinger continued to insist that all of Lawrence was now under copyright again. His firm even proceeded to try to charge Penguin Books, which had long ago published old unedited texts of Lawrence in paperback and had borne the cost of defending the publication of *Lady Chatterley* in court, 7½ percent royalties for publishing the new versions. Older versions of the texts, like the original Penguins, the agent conceded, "might continue to circulate but the Lawrence Estate would insist on the corrupt text being identified with a mark of disapproval."

There is nothing new in all this. London booksellers throughout the eighteenth century, as we shall see, claimed what they called "perpetual rights," even though the clear wording of the 1709 copyright act limited ownership of a text to twenty-eight years. Only a judgment by the House of Lords brought the matter to a momentary end, but publishers and agents have continued to strive for what they consider justice, and the Lawrence texts are only one of a number of similar attempts in recent years to establish new copyright on the basis of new editions of works that continue to sell well. Joyce's *Ulysses* was handled in this way by Random House, which set up a board of distinguished scholars to oversee an elaborate computerized edition supervised by a noted German bibliographer. Here the editorial apparatus occupies the entire left-hand page, the text the right, in a synthetic version of the novel published in 1984 by Garland in three volumes as the true text of *Ulysses*, on which a new copyright could be based. Unfortunately for this enterprise, a scholar at the University of Virginia appeared out of the wilderness filled with the fiery zeal of an Old Testament prophet to denounce the edition as incorrect, corrupt, and totally unlike the *really* true text. All of this set off a godawful scholarly brawl, of the kind that only the most objective hardheaded scholars can create, which completely concealed the clear and obvious fact that there is no such thing as a single true and accurate text of *Ulysses*, or of most other great books. What there *is* is a complicated history of textual change and accident. Somewhere in the dust of this quarrel, unmourned by most, lie the publishers' hopes, despite valiant efforts to salvage something, of controlling *Ulysses* for another fifty years.

These cases, turning on legal concepts though they never actually got to court, reveal the way in which print, copyright law, bibliographical scholarship, and romantic-modernist literary doctrine have combined to construct and make real the true and perfect text. The Platonic text is a print-era conception deriving from the ability of the printing process to reproduce, in a way that manuscripts and oral performance cannot, numerous highly accurate identical copies of the same work.

Copyright legitimates, and is legitimated by, the printed text, and both are reinforced by the romantic idealization of the literary text as a perfect product of the creative imagination, a pure Platonic form emerging shining and crystalline from the mind of the artist creator. Printed text, aesthetic theory, and the legal concept are in turn objectified by scholarly editions in which bibliographic scholars purport to recreate and print the nonexistent "true" text, buttressed by an elaborate scholarly apparatus, by collation of the existing historical texts or by divining the true text through the errors of the actual.

Woven of these threads of gossamer, the true text becomes firmly real, solidly out there. But most of the classic texts have a history of successive forms rather than a single unchanging text, and there is seldom any reason to privilege one text as "truer" than any other. Writers are notorious for continually changing their work, and new publications or performances, especially of plays, introduce variants that may as likely be improvements as corruptions of some hypothetical ideal original. Authors' preferences for one version of the work over another establishes little more than that they prefer it. Even when one text is chronologically the latest, or the earliest (which is the true mark, early or late, of authenticity?), there is no certainty that it is the best. Early forms of Wordsworth poems, for example, are usually felt to be fresher and therefore superior to his revisions, but the latest forms of the Shakespeare plays, as printed in the 1623 Folio, were preferred as more finished for centuries over the earlier quartos. Even today when we know a great deal more about the printing history of the Shakespeare texts, there is, as recent bibliographers have at last admitted, no really convincing reason for treating one version as more authentic than another.

The new Cambridge edition of Lawrence was taking for granted, though pushing to the limits of credibility, the print-based, romantic, copyright supported, bibliographic conception of an absolute and perfect Platonic text. It was, like the true cross, the true Lawrence text, whose few actual changes had magically made the entire text so whole, harmonious and radiant as to establish copyright for another fifty years. The history of the Lawrence texts undercuts these claims totally. The original autograph manuscript of *Sons and Lovers*, for example, crucial for being the first version and written by Lawrence himself, had been severely edited by Edward Garnett to produce the first printed edition. Lawrence had pronounced himself very pleased with what had been done: "You did the pruning jolly well, and I am grateful. . . . I wish I were not so profuse—or prolix." The new Cambridge edition, how-ever, included the excised material and claimed that it contributed to the authenticity of its text.

There are even bigger problems of the same kind. Holroyd and Jobson point out that each of the new Cambridge texts is an eclectic amalgamation of several different versions of the same text, mingling unsystematically and incompletely, on no established principles, some details from early drafts with some later changes, producing a kind of bibliographic monster never imagined by the author and never ex-isting in this form before. And yet this was the true text that was to establish control over *all* the writings of D. H. Lawrence for another half century!

The most conservative of institutions, the law presently offers no challenge to the traditional aesthetics of romantic and modern art centering in the creative genius of the artist and the idealized and perfect form of the artwork. Elsewhere the author may be dying and the work of art crumbling to a mere text, but not in the courtroom. The cases used as examples here are representative, and everywhere the courts, aided by the legislatures, have been eager to extend the dogmas of romantic and modern art: satire can attack and slander with impunity, true art has no utilitarian purpose, the artist is a person of extraordinary powers and entitled to special treatment by society, and the perfect and therefore unchangeable form of the work of art,

like some Keatsian "still unravished bride of quietness," is property
of such a special nature that it cannot be alienated from its creator
or even removed from the site for which it was designed. Apollo himself
seems to speak through our modern legislators, lawyers, judges, and
the United States Registrar of Copyrights, Ralph Oman, who ruled
that not only black-and-white films that had been colored by the computer but genetically engineered life-forms could be patented because
like works of art they had "originality, a certain minimum amount of
creative expression and [were] created by a human being."

By way of one last example of the law's support of traditional aesthetics we might consider the matter of royalties paid to heirs. Lawrence died intestate with effects valued at about £2,500, but within
fifty years, though exact figures are not available, his estate had become "one of the biggest," which was the most Holroyd and Jobson
could get anyone to say. They tried to get a fix on what this might
mean by calculating that it can "reasonably be estimated at well into
six figures per year—the estate of George Orwell being worth around
£100,000 a year, those of C. S. Lewis and A. A. Milne £250,000 a
year, and that of Beatrix Potter over a million pounds a year." The
value of literary estates seems to rise astronomically with careful management after, not before, the death of the author.

Who would complain that Pooh and Peter—a million pounds a
year!—are doing well? But it is heirs and agents, not the writers or
their characters, who really cash in. Orwell's deathbed second marriage and the will that left almost all his estate, which had just been
vastly increased by the acceptance of *1984* by the Book of the Month
Club, to the second wife, provide a model for what Holroyd and Jobson
call copyright situations that are "frequently eccentric." In leaving his
money to a young woman with whom he was barely acquainted, Orwell
almost disinherited the child he had insisted on his first wife, Eileen,
adopting when she was dying of cancer, and nearly ignored his sister,
who had and would take care of the child. No royalty arrangement was

more eccentric that that of W. H. Auden's literary estate, left to his friend Chester Kallman, and then by him shortly afterward to his father, a New York dentist, who soon departed this world, leaving all to his second wife.

When D. H. Lawrence died without a will, the Red Baron's cousin, Frieda von Richthofen, who had left her husband and children to run away with Lawrence and share his tempestuous life, inherited his estate. Lawrence's agent had foresightedly bought out the claims of Lawrence's sisters and his brother for £500 each. When, after marrying the Lawrences' Italian landlord, Angelo Ravagli, Frieda died, the Lawrence literary estate was distributed between her children by her first marriage—which Lawrence had broken up—and the children of Ravagli. Holroyd and Jobson make icily clear what these arrangements have in fact meant: "For the last quarter of a century, whenever one of Lawrence's works was set for an English Literature examination, filmed by a cinema or television company, or bought by some reader in a bookshop, whenever one of his poems or short stories was reprinted by a publisher in an anthology, the royalties went equally to the Weekleys and the Ravaglis."

All of this is scandal and gossip. It doesn't really matter too much who gets the money. Holroyd and Jobson, after all, want all posthumous royalties to go not to American dentists' second wives or the children of adulterous German aristocrats and Italian landlords but to a fund to support living authors, which sounds fine only until you begin thinking precisely about who these living authors might actually be. But the illogicality, not to say impracticality and even immorality, of the whole business creates a certain uneasiness, which starts in the law but carries over to the literary theory that is supported by it. Awkward questions arise. Is the text on which the royalties are paid so absolutely original and unique as to justify the strange situation in which those who had nothing to do with it should control and profit from it? Did the person who wrote it so surely create it out of whole cloth that it should be passed on to those who have never known the artist and have no care for what use is made of the work?

Perhaps the rush of our modern artists to sympathetic legislatures and courts in our litigious times has not been ultimately so profitable as it has appeared. It not only concedes authority on artistic matters to the state, but in an odd way it may well be that the courts in their very generosity to the arts have unwittingly demystified the old romantic and modern conceptions of art, and the privileges based on them, more thoroughly and conclusively than deconstructive criticism or the politics of the counterculture. The shark has pretty teeth and they have shone nowhere more brightly in our time than in the courtroom, where the spirituality of romantic art, the pure creativity of the artist, and the perfection of the unique work of art have gotten mixed up with some really astounding instances of modern greed, vanity, aggressiveness, rapacity, and hypocrisy. The legislatures and the courts have been friendly, none more so, but who needs enemies when your real friends are seen to be grasping literary agents, mass murderers turned authors, trendy bishops with a literary flair, politicians seeking liberal votes, Cambridge graduates who have read the unexpurgated *Lady Chatterley*, twice, publishers of hard porn, the literary people testifying in the *Lady Chatterley* trial, and the loitering heirs of dead authors?

But why not? Here in this vital world, art and literature are not some high abstraction but levers to be used in the struggle for life. Decayed beauty queens become commissioners of culture and pass out patronage to those they decide are true artists. Clever agents and publishers declare that previously printed editions of Lawrence novels now in the public domain may "continue to circulate but the Lawrence Estate would insist on the corrupt text being identified with a mark of disapproval." In the courtroom and on the floor of the legislature, art can be and still is used for familiar purposes like getting votes, punishing enemies, making money, protecting privacy, selling books, media exposure, staying out of jail, finding an apartment. It is equally useful in achieving darker purposes. *Hustler* and its furious crippled publisher find that the law allows them to use satire as a club with which to beat with impunity a sin-fighting preacher by accusing him of incest with his mother in an outhouse. The Sons of Sam after gunning down God alone knows how many unsuspecting lovers petting in cars, helped by ghostwriters, write books telling all the gory details, and, abetted by publishers speaking with shining eyes of Thoreau and Martin Luther King, invoke the rights of the creative artist to keep the royalties that are the appropriate reward for the creative imagination. Only the brave deserve the fair! A wall of steel, 112 feet long and 12 feet high, is thrown across a public space, and when the tenants of the building protest and try to remove the impediment so they can go to lunch, the artist goes to court to contend that any removal from the exact spot where it has become a public nuisance will destroy the wholeness, harmony, and radiance of his site-specific work of art, *Tilted Arc.*

If this is what art has become in the real world in our time, then the more squeamish might understandably say, let it perish as soon as possible! But is there not about it even in the grotesque forms it takes in the courtroom an admirable and inextinguishable vitality? Plagiarism may become as unknown to us as simony, technology may vaporize the printed book, leaving not a rack behind, originality come to seem as quaint as grace or contrition, artists and authors as bizarre as jugglers, deconstruction may torture the text until it is emptied of all mysteries and drained of all meaning, but art will still remain "in midst of other woe / Than ours, a friend to man."

5

Plagiarism and Poetics:

Literature as Property

and Ethos

Nothing is more common, even in our politicized and materialistic time, than to think of literature and the other arts as somehow still largely privileged by society. Literature may comment upon the social world, but it is thought to do so from a superior position that derives from its origin in gnostic powers of the imagination or the Freudian id, or it is thought to use language in some special way that privileges its statements. It may be involved with politics, as it very much is at the present time in a fashionable Marxism and an evangelistic feminism, but it still continues to approach political questions from the privileged, theoretical position of intellectual high culture, uninterested, that is to say, in getting its hands dirty. "Literature and society" is normally still as much an oxymoron as it was for the founders of literature. When the connection of the two is considered it usually takes into account only some mechanical correspondences between social concerns and literary structures—between middle-class interests and the novel, in one famous case, for example, or between twentieth-century alienation and surrealism in another.

But literature plays a much more complex part in the social

construction of reality, and as a result, like all other social things, lives in an extensive and sensitive cultural web in which movement in one part affects all others. Literature was defined and built into the modern world in a social activity that began in the early eighteenth century. Once in the prerogative of kings, poetry was at that time transformed into literature in the emerging capitalist society, where it became, among other things, the product of the work of skilled professionals and the property of the individuals who created it. Property, work, professional skill, and the individual are powerful concepts in modern society, and their identification with literature has provided potent validations of the reality and importance of literary art. Reciprocally, literature has reinforced the importance and the reality of property, work, and the individual by idealizing them as the unique and perfect work of art created by the inspired labors of the imaginative artist. The web of meaning expanded when the courts made socially real some of the major principles of romantic literature by giving them the substance and majesty of the law, and literature in turn provided a conception of the printed book and the true text that supported the law's need for an object sufficiently firm and unique to be copyrighted. Copyright, which has long been one of the major crossroads of art and society, provides a convenient point at which to examine close-up some of the ways in which literature participates in the socially constructed reality and the ways in which it is affected by major conceptual and technological changes.

The concept of copyright could appear only in a print society, since in oral and even manuscript cultures, texts never stabilize sufficiently to become an objective property. The wheel will have come full circle when in some predictable future copyright will disappear as the electronic database destabilizes the individual text once again. But with the setting up of presses throughout Europe in the second half of the fifteenth century, writing in printed form became sufficiently real, and profitable, to be owned. A loose form of copyright appeared in England in 1557, when the rights in perpetuity to print a particular book were given to the printer or publisher who entered the work in *The Stationers' Register,* the official record book of the booksellers' guild, establishing intention to publish. But in England as on the Continent, the ultimate ownership of the printed word lay with the kings. In the ages of the Tudors, Habsburgs, and Bourbons, publishing was an instrument of state and of its monarch, whose power was openly declared in censorship and the assignment of monopoly rights to print and publish certain titles or categories of books, such as Bibles or legal texts, to particular printers and booksellers. Authors, who were usually paid a small amount by the bookseller for total and perpetual rights to their manuscripts—five pounds for *Paradise Lost*—seem to have seldom thought "that the author of a poem or any other piece of writing possessed rights with regard to these products of his intellectual labor. Writing," Martha Woodmansee continues, "was considered a mere vehicle of received ideas which were already in the public domain."

The Act for the Encouragement of Learning by Vesting Copies of Printed Books in the Authors of 1709 recognized and first legalized in Britain authors' rights of ownership over what they had written. It conferred on their work the legal status of capitalism's most sacred category, property, and gave them legal possession of that property for two successive fourteen-year periods. The humble term *copy money* gave place to *copyright,* which appeared first in Blackstone in 1767, suggesting one of the Enlightenment's natural or inalienable human rights. Literature still was not as real as real property, which under common law is owned in perpetuity by its legal possessor, but "the notion that property can be ideal as well as real, that under certain circumstances a person's ideas are no less his property than his hogs and horses," as Woodmansee puts it, transformed writing from service in the palaces of kings and lords to a Lockean product of the labor of an individual and therefore the creator's rightful property. In the eighteenth century, this concept was elaborated in a series of important court cases that gave increasingly precise legal reality and definition, in the words of Mark Rose, to "the proprietary author and the literary work. The two concepts are bound to each other. To assert one is to imply the other, and together, like the twin suns of a binary star locked in orbit about each other, they define the center of the modern literary system."

During the same time, proto-romantic literary theory was developing poetic versions of "the proprietary author and the literary work" that brought the developing legal realities of copyright and literary theory into a mutually supportive relation. Originality was not a matter of much interest through the seventeenth century, but as the most recent historian of plagiarism puts it, during that time "a modern world was printing and distributing itself into existence. Literary 'careers' would be 'made,' and writerly goods would get sold, not because they were skillful variants of earlier ones but because they were original" (Mallon). Samuel Johnson, a writer who learned his trade in the hard school of Grub Street, argued, for example, in a letter to Thomas Warton in 1757, mixing romantic poetics and copyright law, that the author has "a stronger right of property than by occupancy, a metaphysical right, a right . . . of creation, which should from its nature be perpetual." At about the same time, Edward Young in his "Conjectures on Original Composition" (1759) defined the true literary work in a way that was equally congenial to romantic aesthetics and to a statute that assigned ownership of a specific and unique written object: "An *Original* may be said to be of a *vegetable* nature; it rises spontaneously from the vital root of genius; it *grows*, it is not made."

But the romantic-capitalist copyright-creativity cultural constellation that held firm for so long has begun to wobble recently, most noticeably in the effects of new technology. Above every photocopier in every library hangs a warning, to which no one pays the slightest attention, about legal limits on reproducing copyrighted material. The Xerox makes copyright increasingly uneconomic, inefficient, and therefore pointless. And in the near future, as Max Whitby describes it, communications technology already available will make protection of copyright not just difficult but impossible as the individual text or work disappears into the vast "hypertext" of a database, the parts of which can be endlessly moved about and recombined in different configurations.

> The latest reference libraries house no books. Instead their vast collections are stored in digital form on revolving optical and magnetic disks in anonymous warehouses around the world. Their entrance is your telephone. Dial-up databases, as these electronic archives are known, are fast becoming a valuable supplement to more conventional means of research. To exploit the new technology you need [only] a personal computer and a relatively inexpensive gadget called a modem that allows text to be transmitted over an ordinary telephone line. The equivalent of a reader's ticket is a personal password, rather like a bank PIN number, which identifies you to the archive for accounting purposes. Thus equipped, you can call a distant database, enter a query on your keyboard and a few seconds later read the response from the library on your screen display. . . . All the articles you find can be recorded on the home computer and printed out later on for study in depth.

It is not only that this kind of database encourages the avoidance of copyright but that it vaporizes the conception of what Northrop Frye calls the remarkable idea that a "book . . . [is] an invention distinctive enough to be patented." In this kind of database individual texts quickly lose their boundaries and their identity as they are broken up and recombined. Pictures can be stored, mixed with text, and transmitted in the same way. Films, television programs, and music are even more vulnerable to exact reproduction and mixing by VCR and tape recorder. In the shifting sea of images, sounds, and words created by these new technologies—the database, soundbase, pictobase, or

mixed-media base—not only does copyright become difficult to en-
force, but backup romantic concepts like originality, creativity, and
the fixed and distinct work, as in a single book or a picture, are
increasingly at risk.

Stirrings in one part of the web—more efficient copying technology
and different methods for storing information—vibrate with intensified
effects in the other parts affecting such traditional social epistemes as
property, copyright, privacy, individualism, and selves who have inalienable connections with their ideas and words. And as these critical
values have trembled, so has literature, nowhere more obviously than
in the advanced criticism of the cultural left, which has been busy
undermining the concept of literary property from many different an-
gles. The author has been stripped of property rights by being declared
to have died, presumably intestate, and by having been denied the
ownership of texts that are said to have been the products not of
individual creativity but of communal attitudes. If they can be said
to have been made at all, it was by the culture and its language, and
therefore do not belong to any individual. "Language writes, not the
author" is a point of view that reduces the creative individual of
romantic theory into little more than a factory worker assembling images, words, and ideas that are the common property of the culture
and embedded in the language. Copyright is now transferred by criticism from a proprietary author to populist readers by establishing that
the meaning of a text is established by the readers, not by the author
or the work he or she made. At the more radical end of this critical
movement, the literary work is made nearly worthless by devaluing it,
demystifying it, emptying it of meaning, decentering and dispersing
its parts. At the farthest end of the critical spectrum, private property
has been abolished altogether in the literary world by a deconstruction
that vaporizes the work of art into nothingness by focusing on the
inevitable contradictions in what it says and the infinite deferral of the
absolutes on which it pretends to ground its meaning system.

New technology and radical literary criticism are two places at which it is possible to see in some depth how change works in the cultural web, but the extensiveness and the subtleties of interaction are more obvious in a recent literary scandal involving the question of plagiarism.

The White Hotel by D. M. Thomas was published, to considerable acclaim, in London by the old left-wing firm of Victor Gollancz in 1981. The novel is both sensational and serious, telling the tragic story of Elizabeth Erdman, born Morozova, in Kiev to a Russian Jewish father and a Polish Catholic mother, in the late nineteenth century. The novel opens with a stream-of-consciousness autobiographical poem about her unrestrained erotic fantasies, sadomasochistically inclined, of a stay in a Swiss spa, the white hotel, in 1919. It moves on to an analysis with Sigmund Freud, reported in the style of his early studies in hysteria. Psychoanalysis bridges the gap between the dream world of the poetry and the real world, and the narrative becomes increasingly realistic as Morozova becomes an opera singer in Kiev, married to the Jewish director of the opera, until he is killed in a gulag. She goes on caring for his child by a previous marriage until the German army captures Kiev in the autumn of 1941 and sets up a killing machine for many thousands of Jews in the infamous ravine of Babi Yar. Lisa, who could have escaped, stays with the child and goes to the ravine, where both are shot and, after falling into a heap of bodies at the bottom of the ravine, are later mutilated in barbarous fashion. An alternative ending is provided in which Lisa dreams of an afterlife, in either Heaven or Palestine, where she is united again with those she loves; but the happy ending is grimly ironic, a human dream of escape from a hideous reality.

The movement of the book, Thomas himself explained, is from the freedom of pure erotic dream, unhampered by any realistic restraint, at the beginning, to the terrible limitations of the flesh and totally meaningless objectivity at the end, when Lisa and the child are reduced to sodden objects piled thousands upon their thousands in the great ravine of Babi Yar running down to the river at Kiev. This, in Thomas's novel, is a parable of the terrible history of the twentieth century. Pleasure and free play of imagination overwhelmed by pain and the limitations of the flesh—Eros destroyed by Thanatos. The book is shocking, violently, heavily so, both in its explicit details of released libidinal imagination and in its later portrayal of the monstrous ugliness of mass death. A book for our terrifying times, it received considerable and respectful critical attention, particularly for the power with which Lisa's almost unbearably immediate experience of the slaughter at Babi Yar was conveyed.

But then, in the letters section of the *Times Literary Supplement*, beginning March 26, 1982, *The White Hotel* began to get some less welcome attention. The crucial section of the novel describing the horrible events at Babi Yar, D. A. Kenrick wrote to point out, was in large part a word-for-word, or only slightly changed, version of these events by their single survivor, the actress Dina Pronicheva. Her description of the atrocity had been recorded in an interview and published by the Russian writer Anatoli Kuznetsov in his book *Babi Yar*, published first in a cut version in Russia in 1966 but in a full translation by David Floyd in London by Jonathan Cape in 1970. The original edition of *The White Hotel* acknowledges some indebtedness to Kuznetsov and Pronicheva in small print on the copyright page: "I also gratefully acknowledge the use in Part V of material from Anatoli Kuznetsov's *Babi Yar* (New York: Farrar, Straus & Giroux; London: Jonathan Cape, 1970), particularly the testimony of Dina Pronicheva." The word "use" seems a circumlocution, especially in the context of the fulsome acknowledgment of quotation in the same paragraph that the Yeats estate required for a few lines of poetry. Two pages later there is an elaborate "Author's Note," which explains, in much larger print than the *Babi Yar* acknowledgment, just how Thomas used Freud in constructing the study of Lisa's hysteria and commenting on the complex relationship of fact to fiction. But of the debt to Pronicheva and Kuznetsov, there is nothing more.

To put it bluntly, Thomas all but concealed that he had copied verbatim at least four or five pages, far beyond what any court has yet allowed as "fair use," from Pronicheva and Kuznetsov. Furthermore, the pages "used" are, by common agreement, the structural and emotional center of both books, the actual experience when the victim passes the wire, disrobes, and goes forward on a narrow path along the edge of the ravine, where machine guns fired from the other side kill the victims and efficiently drop them of their own weight into the ravine. No one who has read Dina Pronicheva's words can ever forget them, for they have the power of the holy as we have come to know it in our times, the slaughter of the helpless and innocent at the hands of an efficient totalitarian state run by some crazed egomaniacal tyrant in the name of some mad ideology. To handle this kind of material in an improper manner is to risk defilement.

Some sense of this and its connection with traditional literary values was expressed by Kenrick, the man who blew the whistle in the *TLS*, when he remarked that it is deeply wrong for "the author of a fiction [to] choose as his proper subject events which are not only outside his own experience but also, evidently, beyond his own resources of imaginative recreation." Another *TLS* correspondent, the novelist Emma Tennant, wrote that *The White Hotel* gave off, "a distinct whiff of moral unease. . . . Dina Pronicheva was a real human being and the sufferer of these monstrosities. The words given to Thomas's fictional heroine are hers, and no writer has the moral right to take the experience of a real human being and attach it, for his or her own ends, to a made-up character, using the very words of that human being's testimony." As this kind of moral and aesthetic comment continued, certain unattractive words inevitably were heard. For David Frost, "Thomas's use of *Babi Yar* seemed opportunist in a way characteristic of the novel as a whole."

Thomas himself joined the exchange of letters in the *TLS* on April

2, 1982, and while he never denied using *Babi Yar*, he brought himself to speak only of an "indebtedness" that he felt he had openly and adequately acknowledged. He then went on to justify his use of the words of Dina Pronicheva in terms of the structure of his novel, which moves, according to him, "from the infinitely varied world of narrative fiction . . . to a world in which fiction is not only severely constrained but irrelevant." Beginning in dream and poetry, and moving through more and more impersonal forms of discourse, the novel came in the end to brutal and exact realism. At that point, according to Thomas, only a precise use of the actual words of the one survivor of the massacre would do, since by then objective fact had entirely displaced earlier imaginative play. As Lisa's individuality disappears into the pile of bodies in the ravine, so the freedom of dream and poetry and fiction to create an imaginative reality disappears into fact, and "the only appropriate voice becomes that voice which is like a recording camera, the voice of the one who was there."

This is actually an interesting argument intellectually, one that fits tragedy in general—"Cabined, cribbed, confined," "O God, I could be bounded in a nutshell"—and this particular tragic novel rather well. It would, however, have been more acceptable had Thomas refrained from going on verbally to rub his hands like some Dickensian lawyer, "My conscience is easy because in writing my novel, I observed the creative laws which it imposed." His case would have been helped too had he put the borrowed material inside quotes, or acknowledged publicly and specifically that he had "quoted" Kuznetsov, and how much. Or if he had ever asked, which he never did, the publishers and the author for permission to quote the material he unquestionably printed. His "inspirational use," as he brazenly called it, of the *Babi Yar* material would also have been more acceptable had it been accompanied by some concern for Kuznetsov's widow, who, having been left in poor circumstances after her husband's death in 1979, tried, but failed, to get some settlement from Thomas and his publisher.

Thomas's use of the *Babi Yar* material and his refusal to see anything wrong with what he had done are a scandalous instance of a large shift taking place in attitudes toward copyright, creativity, plagiarism, and certain kinds of linked ethical behavior. Thomas never really understood that there was anything wrong, or even odd, about what he had done. As Margaret Scanlan says, "It is easier for [Thomas] to plagiarize Kuznetsov because he has already felt free to appropriate Freud's own real letters—the very touching one about the end of his 'affectional life' with the death of his four-year-old grandson, for example. The whole book is postmodernist (cheaply) in the range of voices and 'discourses' adapted and then dropped, no one carrying authority or seeming to speak for the author." What followed made it clear how far these changes had gone and how intertwined they were with other central cultural values. Those who wrote to the *TLS* were still outraged by what Thomas had done in *The White Hotel*—"no writer has the moral right to take the experience of a real human being and attach it, for his or her own ends, to a made-up character, using the very words of that human being's testimony." And in the larger public scene, plagiarism, the negative side of originality, or the sin against the creative imagination, still remained a word to conjure with. Senator Joe Biden of Delaware was in 1987 forced to withdraw, though with a good deal of puzzled resentment at having somehow been wronged, from the presidential race when it was revealed that he had a long history of plagiarism extending from his student days in law school at Syracuse to campaign speeches in which he used without attribution some words and even biographical details of the leader of the British Labour party, Neil Kinnock. Politicians know about these things, and Kinnock jovially and publicly embraced Biden on their next meeting. But Biden must have sensed that there were still people who might on later occasion hold plagiarism against him. In 1989 the Delaware Supreme Court, for reasons that needed no explanation and got none, took the unusual step of setting up a special commission that absolved Biden of having been a plagiarist in papers he wrote while at law school in upstate New York many years earlier. A bit out of their usual jurisdiction, but still very authoritative should unreasonable charges ever be leveled in some future race for an office of high trust in the Republic!

In 1988–89 Shervert H. Frazier, a distinguished psychologist, was charged with plagiarism in a number of articles he had published in professional journals over the years. The charge was made by a graduate student who had made the discoveries and followed them up while working on his dissertation in the stacks of another university than the one in which Frazier taught. There was, Frazier insisted, no intention to deceive or claim others' work for his own, only confusion in his notes; but the Faculty Conduct Committee of the Harvard Faculty of Medicine recommended his resignation. He complied with considerable embarrassment, but many of those he worked with and other members of his profession came strongly to his defense publicly, attacking the administration and making it clear that they saw nothing very wrong in what he had done.

Our culture is obviously in between two views on this question, and while plagiarism is still one of the few sins, along with racism and sexual harassment, for which colleges and universities will on persistent and egregious provocation dismiss paying students, the matter is becoming more blurry all the time. The dean's office at Princeton, one college among many to do so, takes great care each fall to explain an honor code with an explicit definition of original work and of plagiarism to entering students, and every paper and exam in order to receive credit has to carry a signed honor pledge of originality. But each time a specific case appears, the student protests that he or she didn't understand what was involved, and besides the working notes got mixed up. Some of the more cross-grained faculty members inevitably come forward to testify that plagiarism along with originality is philosophically a discredited concept, and in time the case goes to courts of law where due process has become far more important than passing off someone else's words, if indeed words can any longer belong to someone, as your own.

The publisher of *Babi Yar*, Jonathan Cape, never went to court or brought any pressure to bear on Thomas or on his publisher, most surprising for a publisher since monetary damages could easily have been claimed, and one of the Cape editors, without comparing the texts in detail, declared himself satisfied that no harm had been intended or done. A later edition of *Babi Yar* published by Pocket Books actually carried a blurb reading, "*Babi Yar*, the extraordinary story that inspired D. M. Thomas' world-renowned bestseller, *The White Hotel*." It is hard not to believe after reading this that in the New York and London publishing houses and the more fashionable scenes of writing in the West End, plagiarism by the 1980s was no longer a really serious issue. Ian McEwan provides what is probably an accurate description of the situation: "There are many novelists who feel that books, particularly fictions, are as legitimate a part of their total experiences as sex or death, and their work is drenched in their reading."

Something like the same attitudes increasingly appear to prevail in the intellectual world at large. After the *White Hotel* scandal broke, the editors of the *TLS* asked a number of experts on art and copyright to participate in a printed discussion of whether copyright and plagiarism were still living ideas. Their responses were published under the heading "Plagiarism—A Symposium" in the April 9, 1982, issue. Not one of the experts, let it be said at once, explicitly condemned Thomas or *The White Hotel*. They did not praise the novel or what the author had done, nor did they approve of plagiarism, but they felt the matter to be more a question of manners than one of law and ethics. "Probably the most wounding insult," John Sutherland remarked, "one can level at a self-respecting author is 'plagiarist,' suggestive as it is of underhand theft and impotence." Ian McEwan forcefully described the long-standing connection between romantic aesthetics and morality, but in a way that made clear that the old relationship had pretty much disappeared, leaving plagiarism only a matter of aesthetics: "In our literary tradition, with its powerful emphasis on the uniqueness of the individual imagination, to be a plagiarist is to be fundamentally dishonest, it is to claim as uniquely yours what is uniquely someone else's and is a tacit admission that your own imagination is defective, insufficient to sustain its own peculiar hold on the world. What is the point of you if you cannot think things up for yourself?"

It wasn't just a matter of no longer taking a strict view of copyright, or its illegitimate brother, plagiarism. Those ideas were not only becoming less important, they were ceasing to exist. Part of the ontological slippage occurred in the area of a pervasive historical relativism, characteristic of our time, that perceived copyright not as a legal manifestation of a universal or eternal fact but only as the product of a particular place and time. And having appeared at one time, it might well disappear at another. Wilfrid Mellers, a historian of music and specialist in folk music, cautioned that we "remember that the concept [of copyright] is not absolute, but socially conditioned." Lord Goodman, a historian of the law as well as a noted jurist in the field of copyright, told us that in the Roman law "there is not a single word to suggest that an author or artist could be entitled to prevent the multiplication of copies of his work or to prevent others from public performance, adaptation or any other use—whether fair or unfair." It was, he went on, "several centuries [before] the idea grew up that a man should earn something from his writing, music, or from the reproduction of his paintings. The commercial exploitation of the brainchildren of others was viewed with complete composure by the entire world, including, weirdly enough, the majority of the creative artists who were so despoiled."

Copyright is based on the assumption that the work protected is sufficiently original and unique to constitute a distinct written object differing significantly from all other written objects. Originality and uniqueness are therefore as crucial to copyright law as to romantic aesthetics, but their reality has been dimming for some time. Cultural anthropology, for example, has taken away their universality by demonstrating that originality is not much cultivated in primitive societies, where the norm remains repetition with limited variation rather than creation of something new. Like all educated people, a number of the *TLS* panelists were well aware of the anthropological viewpoint and brought it to bear on Western society to show that when we look closely, imitation has been far more a factor in letters, and even more so in music, as in the extensive borrowings of Bach and Handel, than is usually acknowledged. Once the door was opened, the closet of literary borrowing turned out to be filled with illustrious names and books. The Jacobean dramatist John Webster mined Montaigne, Daniel Defoe lifted anything that came his way, Coleridge's "inspirational use" of German philosophers is still a barely concealed scandal, Charles Reade stole from Trollope, Scott Fitzgerald from his poor mad wife, Zelda, F. R. Leavis borrowed from Queenie. Norman Mailer's novel of fact, *Marilyn*, was "one of the literary heists of the century," according to Maurice Zolotow, but not much more than what Alex Haley was accused of doing in *Roots*, for example. Artists have been "in each other's pockets all the time," says McEwan, who then adds, "and not always dishonestly either."

What was concealed earlier is openly acknowledged, flaunted even, in modern art. Mellers calls it an art of inspired theft, "Pound's pillage of the past, Joyce's multi-layered cultural and social strata, Brecht's identification of poet and people, Burroughs's exploitation of the collage and cut-out." This is the art of a world where theft, imitation, and borrowing shade into the general condition assumed to be normative by structuralism in which not only art but the entire social world is an artifact assembled from the bits and pieces of "our polyglot world, our global village in which both time and space are interfused, [where] layers of experience . . . coexist." We "live vicariously, in a museum culture," Mellers goes on, and "the museum has grown so vast that it has few limits temporal or geographical. In any given artefact everything depends on how far our confusion is illuminated, if not ordered: on what is done with the objects borrowed or stolen from the museum." *Finnegans Wake* provides a perfect example and description of this kind of what it calls "stolentelling": "Every dimmed letter in it is a copy and not a few of the silbils and wholly words I can show you in my kingdom of Heaven. The lowquacity of him! With his threestar monothong! Thaw! The last word in stolentelling! And what's more rightdown lowbrown schisthematic robblemint!"

In a world where words and things are so protean as this, copyright and plagiarism, originality and uniqueness, individualism and creativity, empty out their reality to become only ideology. The disintegration of these concepts has been hastened by a widely accepted Marxist sociology that has explained the appearance in the eighteenth century of copyright laws and the linked artistic ideas like creativity and originality as a conversion of what Sutherland calls "things of the mind into transferable articles of property. . . . [which] has matured simultaneously with the capitalist system." It has always seemed something less than entirely natural and inevitable that anyone could appropriate the common language and common ideas as property, just as there is now real doubt about the copyrighting of basic computer software systems and of organisms and animals produced by genetic research. In the face of these persistent doubts, the concept of literary property had to be reinforced, McEwan tells us, and was further legitimated by giving it a psychological base in the creative imagination of the artist. "Originality became a *ne plus ultra* and the pearl that was certainly not without price . . . as a part of a psychological process that was also sociological and economic. In a producer-consumer society, the producer must protect his rights; and calls on moral rights in doing so. Even if he who steals my wares may be stealing trash, his theft may threaten my livelihood."

But the psychological underpinnings of creativity, copyright, and plagiarism are no longer so firm as they once were. "The faculties of creativity and originality have come to seem less, and those of imitation, repetition and variation more the norm of psychic activity," says the most psychoanalytical of the experts on the plagiarism panel, Harold Bloom. He quotes Emerson that even "the originals are not original," and evokes the myth of myths, "that one poet wrote all the poems, that one storyteller told all the stories." Originality is for Bloom only a dream which the modern artist, with an Oedipal need to create something new and different from the father-predecessor's work, pursues in an endless "anxiety of influence," never "certain precisely when he is quoting," original only in the "belated" and self-conscious modern sense of misreading those he is unavoidably plagiarizing, making lucky mistakes when he is trying to copy them down, culpable only when he steals from second-rate writers.

In Bloom's psychology, everything blurs into everything else, and copyright and creativity and originality are only mad dreams of freedom. Plagiarism is the human condition. Not all the other contributors to the symposium are so apocalyptic as Bloom, but he provides the myth, as it were, that explains how copyright and plagiarism, along with creativity and originality, are fading out of existence: "For the legally untrained mind there is something mysterious in copyright. An immaterial property right, it inheres in a perfect, Platonic idea of the 'work' which elusively transcends any possible book (or otherwise reproduced) version" (Sutherland).

There has, it turns out, always been "something mysterious in copyright" for legally trained minds as for the minds of lay people. Courts have consistently had the greatest difficulty in practice and in theory of distinguishing with any precision the essential element that is protected against infringement by copyright. "Wherein consists the identity of a book?" was a question asked in a famous copyright case, *Millar v. Taylor*, as long ago as 1769, and copyright law has never satisfactorily answered the question, "What is protected?" The distinguished professor of copyright law in the Harvard Law School Justin Kaplan takes us through the many ways copyright has been defined in his *Unhurried View of Copyright.* The ideas, expression, style, title, story, and character have all been proposed at one time or another as the essential objects protected by copyright. But still the questions have multiplied in forms so twisted and perverse as to sound like modern paradoxes of Zeno. Are Wonderwoman and Batman infringements on the Superman copyright? How much constitutes the elusive "fair use?" Can facts be copyrighted, such as dictionary definitions, collections of biographical information, maps, or reports of events? Do abridgments and translations constitute copies of a work, and if so what is it that is abridged and translated? Does a transformation into a different medium, such as a play or film, transfer some essence from the original to the new form? Are there subjects too big for copyright, such as mixed marriages, which the owners of the popular play of the 1920s, *Abie's Irish Rose*, once claimed in court as exclusively their own property? Are there subjects too small?

J. O. Urmson in his contribution to the symposium on copyright expressed a general feeling on the part of the panelists that plagiarism is only a bare legality which on a more meaningful level can not be distinguished from other writing activities: "What is plagiarism, apart from legal questions of ownership, copyright or financial gain? How, for example, does it differ from repetition, reportage, quotation, paraphrase, exposition and other ways of reproducing previously existing material?" As its reality fades, its moral dimensions contract. One wouldn't want to do it, at least in the ordinary way, but does it really matter very much any more? "Plagiarism," Urmson sighed, "is closer to pride, a sin of the spirit, than to the criminal activities of the burglar." In this kind of bathos did literature die.

6

Technology and Literature:

Book Culture and

Television Culture

At different times in human history different forces, now changes in the climate, then surges of religious energy, have affected cultural values and the social arrangements that instrument them. In the modern West, technology has increasingly provided the energy and direction for cultural change. Witold Kula has, for example, in *Measures and Men*, described the way in which standardized weights and measures completely reorganized social life and remade the way agriculture and commerce were managed. Clocks, too, as David S. Landes shows in *Revolution in Time: Clocks and the Making of the Modern World*, changed life and thought with an accurate and increasingly cheap machine that directly changed the ways almost all things were done, from measuring the longitude to calculating speed. In our time, as the pace of technological change has increased, *the* bomb, *the* pill, the automobile, computer, and television have radically affected everything from international relations and sexual morality to where people live and the way in which they conceive of their own mental processes.

126

But technological change now comes in different ways than it once did. As a manufacturing society has become a service society, communications has increasingly replaced industrial production as the central business of the society. "The major modern communication systems are now so evidently key institutions in advanced capitalist societies that they require the same kind of attention . . . that is given to the institutions of industrial production and distribution" (Raymond Williams, 1976). Labor now "takes the form of men and women acting on other men and women, or, more significantly, people acting on information and information acting on people" (Poster). And as communications has become the primary mode of production and the condition of labor, change has become less mechanical, with one thing directly pushing another, and more a matter of information flow. Using the old mechanical model, we might say, for example, that the photocopier by providing numerous cheap copies of a printed work makes copyright less enforceable, and as copyright weakens the traditional views of individual creativity and originality that had it had legitimated cease to be practical and therefore believable. An informational model of social change would reveal, however, without concern for priority, that the photocopier, weak copyright, structuralist poetics, new-style democratic politics, and numerous other social energies are all "saying" that texts are not so unique and particular as was once thought, or, more positively, that things of all kinds are much the same. In this new informational context, older views of copyright, originality, and artistic creativity would begin to lose plausibility and in time would simply disappear.

The great changes that have come to literature in recent years in the midst of a transition from a print to an electronic culture seem to be better explained by the informational model of change than a mechanical one. In the 1950s and early 1960s such books as Harold Innis, *The Bias of Communication*, Marshall McLuhan, *The Gutenberg*

Galaxy, and Eric Havelock, *Preface to Plato*, advanced the argument that the dominant mode of communication doesn't just change the way things are done but restructures consciousness. "The medium is the message" is the way McLuhan famously put the view that each of the major historical information technologies—oral, written, printed, and electronic—has modified perception and posited a different kind of "truth." Oral societies seek wisdom, manuscript and print societies knowledge and information, and, now, electronics manipulate bytes to produce data. The Greek world was transformed—philosophy for poetry, Plato for Homer—in the fifth century B.C. by the appearance of writing in an oral society, and the Western world was transformed again by the appearance of print in the mid-fifteenth century. And in the late twentieth century print culture is giving way to an electronic culture that stores and transmits information by means of such electric devices as the telegraph, telephone, radio, television, and computer.

Primary modes of communication and information storage do not change all at once, or altogether. Orality is always a prominent feature of human society. In the age of manuscripts, society as a whole was still primarily oral, and when books were still few, the available texts were still read like manuscripts, numinous, magical in their physical being like the early Bibles. Wisdom came from poring over them again and again, reading with the intensity that produced, for example, Jewish Midrash or the biblical commentary of the Christian Church Fathers. "From the Middle Ages until sometime after 1750," according to Robert Darnton (1986) "men read 'intensively.' They had only a few books—the Bible, an almanach, a devotional work or two—and they read them over and over again, usually aloud and in groups, so that a narrow range of traditional literature became deeply impressed on their consciousness."

Change in the way trustworthy information is acquired comes slowly and incompletely, and involves great personal and social anxiety. Plato's philosophy, its subtle distinctions and abstract conceptions, were, in ways Eric Havelock has shown, the products of alphabetic writing, which was replacing oral discourse in fifth-century Greece as the dominant mode of knowledge. The Socratic dialogues record the intense anxieties generated by this radical cultural change, which in Athens led to the execution of the philosopher representing the new written point of view. The situation was more highly charged for being a transitional one in which Socrates made his points in talking situations, dialogues in which points were argued in the manner of public debate and conversation, which were then recorded in writing by his pupil Plato. In a number of the dialogues, it was even argued that writing endangers knowledge since it offers no opportunity for dialectic questioning and clarification.

Many centuries later, at the end of a manuscript culture long accustomed to accept the authority of the written, John Trithemius (1462–1516), an abbot in charge of one of the last scriptoria, felt that the written word was always more meaningful than the printed: "As the scribe is copying the approved texts he is gradually initiated into the divine mysteries and miraculously enlightened. Every word we write is imprinted more forcefully on our minds since we have to take our time while writing and reading."

But change does come, and while all past modes of information and communication remain simultaneously in play, the new mode comes to dominate as the most useful, reliable, and, in time, truthful way of getting information. The print revolution began in the mid-1400s, and print began to affect culture at once, producing, in place of the few books that the scriptoria produced—a scribe is said to have been able to copy only one or two books a year—between ten and fifteen thousand different titles, or, at the minimal runs of five hundred copies (Aldus had some runs as high as three thousand), up to 7.5 million books in the fifty years after 1450. The cultural effects of printed books, such as legal codes and vernacular Bibles, were obvious at once, but the old oral-scribal society was not fully transformed to a print culture until the eighteenth century. It was only then, by way of small but revealing instances, that common articles like theater tickets, marriage licenses (Pamela could not have proved her "vartue" with "marriage lines," which were not available until the 1750s), and indentures began to be printed, indicating print's extension into all areas of ordinary life. Printing, generating its own markets, "took off," as the economists say, during the eighteenth century, as newspapers and magazines became familiar, the overt restraints of censorship disappeared, professional writers for a public marketplace appeared, and printing houses in London grew from the 20 allowed when the Licensing Act lapsed in 1695 to 124 by 1785. Figures from the recent *Eighteenth-Century Short Title Catalogue*—kept in a computer data base and on microfiche, not, ironically, printed!—show that the number of English titles printed in England doubled—along with presses, printers, and booksellers—during the eighteenth century, going from 9,267 in the decade ending 1710 to 20,068 in the decade ending 1800 (Mitchell).

By the eighteenth century printed materials were so widespread as to bring on fear of a "literacy crisis," a literacy crisis which was the exact opposite of ours in that it involved too much rather than too little reading. There is a continuing, and unresolvable, argument about the actual increase in literacy rates in the eighteenth century, but the leaders of society then certainly feared that reading had become much too widespread, and the dangers of increased reading by the lower classes were much discussed. Locke did not, for example, favor teaching the poor, and others even less broad-minded considered ignorance as the opiate that a benign Providence had given the lower classes to dull their misery. Reading came to be feared in much the same way that too much television viewing in late twentieth-century America has become a kind of cultural bogey. "Those who deplored [reading] did not simply condemn its effects on morals and politics; they feared it would damage public health. A 1795 tract listed the physical consequence of excessive reading: 'susceptibility to colds, headaches, weakening of the eyes, heat rashes, gout, arthritis, hemorrhoids, asthma, apoplexy, pulmonary disease, indigestion, blocking of the bowels, nervous disorder, migraines, epilepsy, hypochondria, and melancholy'" (Darnton 1986).

But nothing stopped the spread of reading, and by 1800, Darnton tells us, "men were reading 'extensively.' They read all kinds of material, especially periodicals and newspapers, and read it only once, then raced on to the next item." In this vast increase of reading and printing, Western Europe was transformed from an oral to a print society. As the writing-reading, in contrast to the talking-listening, interaction became more commonplace, and more a crucial part of the life of the individual, the consciousness of at least the intellectual and reading classes was being reshaped by the new way of getting reliable information.

In conversation, the people involved are face to face, interacting and constantly adjusting to one another to insure understanding. On public occasions, each listener's understanding is guided by the speaker and by others in the audience, which tends to rule out eccentric, individual reactions in favor of more normative responses. Reading, by its nature, however, makes for the private, inward-turned self, the separated individuals who make up modern society's "lonely crowd." Orality reinforces communal, public life, favors the outgoing personality, and it makes for group conformity. Oral life is tribal life, reading makes for modern society made up of separate individuals, what electronic life will be we are only beginning to glimpse.

In Gutenberg society reading is first of all a useful, even a necessary, skill, but the intensity of the experience of learning to read, culminating in the red letter day, unforgotten by most, when we are certified as able to read, suggests how central reading has been to the modern psyche. To be acknowledged as able to read is an initiation rite, as it were, into the human condition, full acceptance into the

Gutenberg tribe. It is from writing and reading that Gutenberg people not only get information but find out who and where they are. Readers are isolated individuals, encapsulated in silence, their intelligence encountering on the printed page a removed and mysterious reality that appears not *en clair* but as a set of abstract symbols, not pictographs but alphabetic signs representing a spoken language that is itself only arbitrarily and conventionally related to reality. The printed signs are indeterminate and require endless interpretation. Lacking the full context of oral situations, truth is never simple in print but always ambivalent, uncertain, elaborate, complex as the grammar and syntax out of which sentence and paragraph are constructed. As Walter Ong (1988) says, "You cannot ever make [written] language come out even, . . . it conceals as well as reveals, and does so by its very design."

Print, through reading, not only helped to shape the dominant modern character type, inward, alienated, puzzled, Hamlet or Ivan Karamazov, it also inevitably exerted pressure on the intellectual institutions of modern society as well. Philosophy in the age of print, from Descartes and Bacon to Ayer and Derrida, by way of obvious example, has concerned itself almost exclusively with the epistemological issues that became of first importance when the reading situation became the standard setting of understanding. The problematics of knowledge that modern philosophies like structuralism and deconstruction assume are built into the print perspective, and evaporate like the morning dew in another medium. Literature was even more print's creature, down to the smallest details. Its authors became real in the world and to themselves by virtue of books that printed their names on the title page, thus objectifying their identity as writers. The emphasis on the fine details of style that has characterized literature from the beginning is possible only with a stable printed text—imagine trying to follow a pattern of images, a series of linked ironies, a pattern of symbols in an oral performance! The close intense reading, and rereading, of a stable and highly styled text that have in one way or another been the central interpretive methods of literature are feasible only because the printing press has fixed a definite text in numerous exact copies of identical books. "Structure" becomes conceivable and visible only in a text that print has spatialized and made observable as a whole. The bibliographic ideal of a "true" text is a literary offshoot of printing house proofs and the ideal of total accuracy and regularity encouraged by printing house practices. The conception of a universal literature, romanticism's imaginary library, becomes possible only in the huge collections of printed books that have collected in the great modern libraries the imaginative writings of all places and times.

Print literally made literature, as I have detailed in an earlier work, *Samuel Johnson and the Impact of Print*, and the literary transformations of print logic could be enumerated almost endlessly, but the main point is clear enough. So central has print been to literature that it is no exaggeration to say that literature has historically been the literary system of print culture. At the level of the obvious, literature has been more than anything else a collection of canonical works, some originally oral or manuscript, but now all printed books—*The Iliad, The Aeneid, The Divine Comedy, Hamlet*. At a deeper level, the deep subject of modern literature has been the difficulty of understanding not unlike that of a reader turning over the pages of a book trying to see through the words to the meaning of the world. Readers are rarely the principal figures of literature, Cervantes's Quixote and Nabokov's Kinbote are exceptions, but the lovers, travelers, invalids, socialites, and sea captains who are our literary heroes experience life in the way that readers experience reality on the printed page, incomplete, mysterious, resistant to any easy or total interpretation, finally escaping judgment. All our older literary genres were originally oral—epic, theater, lyric—but as they were printed and became a part of literature, criticism imputed to them, Sophocles or Molière for example, the complexity and indeterminacy characteristic of literature. Simplicity and literature are mutually excluding terms in a canon built around writers of depths and shadows like Wordsworth and Kafka. Literary being is always subject as in Henry James to another "however," to another thought as in Proust, or to another character and story as in Dickens. The meaning it ultimately seeks, though never finds, is not the fact of things, the identity of the murderer in the detective story, but some possibility that can only be "finely" intuited from the facts. Such a literature has required and received an extensive body of critical interpretation, which starts as interpretation but ends ultimately as indeterminate in itself as the poems and novels it attempts to explain.

Literature, then, realizes in art the condition of consciousness, the epistemological situation implicit in the printed page and the act of reading. And so long as print remained the dominant mode of communication, constantly asserting that knowledge is complex, ambivalent, abstract, the uncertain interpretation of ambiguous signs, a literature built on the same assumptions flourished. But as George Steiner (1985) puts it, "We are now seeing, all of us today, the gradual end of the classical age of reading. Of an age of high and privileged literacy, of a certain attitude toward books which, very roughly, lasted from, say, the period of Erasmus to the partial collapse of the middle-class world order . . . and of the systems of education and values we associate with it." We begin to hear of the need for a history of the book—*Histoire du livre* is now an important category of cultural history in France—and of reading, as if the era of the book had passed its zenith and we could now look back on heroes of reading. Readers who thought they could read their way back through the error of a fallen world to the primal garden knowledge of God and his world, like Ambrose reading, to Augustine's astonishment, without moving his lips, Montaigne finding reality in his tower library, and Milton reading until blind and then being read to by family and friends. We shall not see the likes again of Doctor Johnson, who as a young man "read like a Turk," or even such fictional readers as Mr. Bennett, who retreated to his library to escape the pressures of the household in *Pride and Prejudice*. The buildings of the book, the great libraries and colleges, begin to look quaint, like medieval cathedrals, and become inefficient and uneconomic. The setting of privacy and silence reading requires becomes harder to find. The great social issues the printed book provoked, literacy, censorship, originality, pornography, plagiarism, copyright, freedom of expression, are, after a final flare-up, beginning to look illusory.

Humanism's long dream of learning, of arriving at some final truth by enough reading and writing, is breaking up in our time. Science is untroubled, but the possibility of knowing the individual and the social world that has driven the humanities and the social sciences since the late Middle Ages is dissipating, leaving us with, as Liam Hudson says, "something . . . enduringly melancholy: an academic landscape that lacks an adequate foundation in the truth." Hudson is specifically describing the breakup in contemporary psychology of the belief that progress is being made in the understanding of the mind, one of humanism's most important adventures. But his powerful portrayal of the realization that there has been something deeply wrong with the entire effort can well stand for the disenchantment in other fields as well at the end of the Gutenberg era. "While outwardly respectable, like Trollope's Barchester, the self-consciously scientific tradition in psychology emerges . . . as a venue dominated by shabby scholarship and creative scandal-mongering; objectivity becomes a slogan, probity a trick of the light. . . . the discipline is not a society of good men and true which harbours the occasional malefactor, but one in which the wilful promotion of one view of reality at the expense of all others is the norm. Psychology is fated, it seems, to serve as one of society's ideological tiltyards. . . . Obviously, it is pointless to pretend that psychology is even a proto-science."

As if to make visible the ending of the era of the book and of reading, large numbers of books are literally disappearing before our eyes from the shelves of those monuments of print culture, the great research libraries. It has long been known that the pulp paper made after about 1870 disintegrates over a period of time because the alum-rosin that helps it take ink evenly combines with moisture to form an acid that breaks down the binding between the pulp fibers. Many presses, like the publisher of this book, are now using acid-free paper, and the deterioration can be halted by a difficult process of deacidification, and some of the books can be saved by being microfilmed. But these remedies are both so labor-intensive and expensive as to make it possible to save only a relatively few of the many books at risk. "For the rest it is too late," Eric Stange concludes. "At least 40 percent of the books in major research collections in the United States will soon be too fragile to handle." A 1987 statistical evaluation of the books in Yale's Sterling Memorial Library confirmed this apocalyptic view, reporting that a survey of "more than 36,500 volumes showed that 37% of the books had brittle paper (i. e. paper which broke after two double folds) and that 83% had acidic paper (i. e. having a pH of below 5.4)." The fact is, the report pronounced, that "all book repositories are self-destructing time bombs."

Economics as well as chemistry seems to be favoring the electronic future over the printed past. The cost of books, as well as the expense of cataloging and handling them in libraries, has been rising for years at inflationary rates. Cheap books and well-kept public libraries were, like careful carpentry and detailed masonry, products of a low-wage, modest-expectation society. They will inevitably disappear in the modern democratic social-welfare state with its constant high inflation rates, union work rules, minimum wages, and costly benefits. The federal government has begun to tax unsold inventories of published books in a way that makes it uneconomic for commercial publishers to keep printed books in stock past the end of any tax year. The great publishing houses associated with bibliographic high culture, Scribner's most recently, have been disappearing or, like Knopf, being combined by takeovers and conglomerations into more profitable communications empires and other types of holding companies. The small bookstore is being replaced by the big high-volume shopping-center chain, like Waldenbooks and B. Dalton. Books proliferate in this big corporation setting, but costs rise, quality and range narrow, low-sales types of books are eliminated, and the half-life of all books is sharply curtailed. Unsold books go quickly to that sad limbo of the book, the remainder house, or to the shredding machine to save warehousing costs and taxes on inventory.

What this means for the book as it has traditionally been written, published, marketed, and read is spelled out in James Kaplan's description of the communications empire that will result from the merger of Time, Inc., with Warner Communications in 1990. "Theoretically, this unprecedented corporate fusion makes it possible for a title to be published in hard-cover by Little, Brown (a division of Time, Inc.), featured as a Book-of-the-Month Club [also owned by Time] main selection, reviewed in Time magazine, issued in paperback by Warner Books, made into a major motion picture by Warner Bros. and turned into a TV series by Warner Television." This might look like only an improvement in publishing efficiency, "the American Dream . . . a company strong enough to be a dominant force in the global media marketplace," but the results are commodities carefully crafted for sale in a specified market. "The very concept of the book as an object to be lingered over and palpated, something that seeps into the soul, has changed. The printed, bound book itself now represents one stage in a process which turns out that most unliterary of all quantities: product."

Though the older books may be disintegrating on the library shelves, it is important to be clear that there is no question of reading or of printed materials disappearing. If there is an alarming dearth of one kind, there is an equally alarming glut of another: "In 1950, when the impact of television first began to be felt, 11,022 books were published in the United States. In 1970, when the impact of the computer began to reach major proportions, the number of books had risen to 36,071. In 1979, after almost thirty years of television and ten years of major computer use, 45,182 books were published in the United States. Book publishing revenues in the United States in 1950 were less than $500 million; in 1970 they were more than $2.9 billion; in 1980, more than $7.0 billion" (Lacey). In new forms of computer printouts and desktop publishing, microfilm and microfiche, laser disks storing millions of words, computer databases containing masses of information in readable form, as well as in magazines, newspapers, and conventional books, the flood of print continues and grows.

It may well be that the Gutenberg age will come to an end, not in the kind of absence of books that Huxley predicts for the future in *Brave New World*, where there is only a single copy of Shakespeare left, but in a bibliographic surplus of the kind that Diderot foresaw at the beginning of the high days of print. In that book of books, the *Encyclopédie*, and in his article on that subject, Diderot already worried openly that the printing press in time would turn out so many books saying so many things that knowledge would become first difficult and then impossible.

> As long as the centuries continue to unfold, the number of books will grow continually, and one can predict that a time will come when it will be almost as difficult to learn anything from books as from the direct study of the whole universe. . . . The printing press, which never rests [will fill] huge buildings with books [in which readers] will not do very much reading, but will instead devote themselves to investigations which will be new, or which they will believe to be new (for if we are even now ignorant of a part of what is contained in so many volumes published in all sorts of languages, they will know still less of what is contained in those same books, augmented as they be by a hundred—a

thousand—times as many more). . . . And eventually the world of learning—our world—may drown in books.

That day appears to have arrived, at least in the scholarly and scientific world, in ways described by Jennifer Kingson in a recent article, "Where Information Is All, Pleas Arise for Less of It." She describes a situation in which "the multiplicity of mediocre publications makes it impossible to sift out the ones that contain fresh ideas. The proliferation of books and journals seems to have narrowed access to information instead of widening it, and some universities [Harvard Medical School is her example] are considering ways to encourage their faculty members to publish less, not more." The information problem is accompanied by a storage problem, in which "the Library of Congress, which holds more that 88 million items . . . receives 31,000 new books and journals a day and keeps 7,000 of them." The new British Library at Saint Pancras to open in 1993 contains eight *miles* of shelves but is still faced with sifting its collections, storing some materials elsewhere, and giving up the long-cherished Gutenberg ideal of a collection containing all printed books. Even with these adjustments, the estimate is that there is in the new building only ten years' space. The problem is general, and only by storing printed material on optical disks and microfilm do librarians hope to avoid running out of shelf space in the next few years. In the long run the answer can only be huge collections of books in central databases, which will, in ways considered in the previous chapter, change the nature of the information stored in them. But such is the tyranny of custom, that librarians go on building libraries and extensions that are out of date even before they are funded.

This is the bizarre way that things die in a society of surplus and overproduction. The end of the age of the book, and with it the age of literature, is figured not only in the difficulties of using and storing printed material, and in the amount of printed material being piled up, but in the gradual waning of the privileged position in the world of knowledge—"what is printed is true"—that the book has held for about five hundred years. As people write and read less, while watching television and using telephones, computers, and other visual and aural electronic modes of communication more and more, reading books is ceasing to be the primary way of knowing something in our society. As the number of expensive journals in the sciences continue to increase, "scientists rely on them less and less. The latest ideas in science are typically exchanged well in advance of formal publication, at conferences and through advance copies of papers distributed by fax machines and computer networks" (Kingson). More than half of my students were already telling me in the mid-1980s that what they saw on a computer screen had more truth for them than did a printed page. Generalizing from the results of a recent federal study of the group of young Americans who graduated from high school in 1972, Clifford Adelman of the U.S. Department of Education concluded that "the 'closing of the American mind' arguments over whether students at elite colleges are required to read Henry James or James Baldwin are irrelevant and effete," since the class of '72, and all since then, spent more of "its academic time learning how to use audio-visual equipment or to organize recreation activities than to read *either* Henry James or James Baldwin." One out of five students in this cohort, which entered primary school in 1960, eventually took a college degree, and while "a significant number [of these] required remedial work in writing or reading, a much larger percentage took courses in oral communication skills, including those with titles such as 'Hello, Then What?' 'Assertiveness' and 'Getting to Know You.'" The control of knowledge, Adelman concludes, "whether verbal or digital—that is the direct result of reading and the manipulation of symbols, is no longer of interest to or available to even the educated portion of the generation presently reaching forty." "Oral communication and psychomotor skills" is what they studied and what continues to engage them.

The reading rooms and stacks of the great research libraries are ceasing to be the definitive scenes of knowledge, and the single figure sitting alone, silently reading to himself or herself less and less the image of human beings acquiring knowledge. The waning of book culture has appeared most dramatically in what has been called "the literacy crisis." This term was first coined in the 1960s to indicate a sharp decrease in the linked language skills of reading and writing, and there are still sharp disagreements about how serious the problem is. The facts are hard to come by, for the numbers vary wildly, as might be expected in connection with something so personal and closely involved with social status as the ability to read well. A survey conducted by the U.S. Census Bureau in 1982, based on a literacy test given to 3,400 adults and described as extremely easy, found that 13 percent of American adults are illiterate. The *New York Times* (September 7, 1988) reports that "the most widely held estimate is that from 23 million to 27 million adults, nearly 10 percent of the nation's population, cannot read and write well enough to meet the basic requirements of everyday life." But the same article adds that "the United States has an official literacy rate of 99 percent," and figures published by the Office of Educational Research (OER) in 1987 paint a picture of improving literacy in the schools in rudimentary and basic reading skills, largely because of improved reading skills of black and Hispanic students. But in the categories that the OER describes as "adept" ("able to find, understand, summarize, and explain relatively complicated literary and informational material") and "advanced" ("able to understand the links between ideas even when those links are not explicitly stated and to make appropriate generalizations even when the texts lack clear introductions or explanations"), the statistics and the trend are not encouraging. Seventeen-year-olds, all groups, white, black, and Hispanic, reading at the adept level went from 37 percent of the total in 1970–71, to 36 percent in 1974–75, 35 percent in 1979–80, and in an unexplained and questionable surge to 39 percent in 1983–84. In this group white literacy showed more severe reductions than it did in the black and Hispanic groups. At the "advanced" level, which is really not very sophisticated by traditional standards for seventeen-year-olds with ten or eleven years of schooling behind them, the drop was from a shockingly low 5 percent in 1970–71, to 3.5 percent in 1974–75, 3 percent in 1979–80, and then, that odd jump again, to 5 percent in 1983–84.

Among those who can read, various surveys may disagree on precise figures, but all accept that the amount of reading, particularly of books, is steadily diminishing. Something like 60 percent of adult Americans apparently never read a book, and most of the rest read only one book a year on the average. In spite of the widely accepted view that Britain is a more literate society, the numbers there are equally startling. At the Book Marketing Council's 1988 annual conference, the British Market Research Bureau in a survey, *Books and the Consumer*, reported that almost three-quarters of the British public buy no books and that in 1985 only 46 percent claimed to read "at least an hour a week."

The numbers differ so widely in the many various samplings of literacy—some even contend that literacy has not decreased—that it may well be that literacy is one of those many things that, contrary to the usual simple faith in numbers, can neither be defined precisely nor counted exactly. The issue is not clarified by virtue of having become a political bone between the liberal left and the conservative right. Those committed to the changing of traditional methods of study and discipline in the schools have been anxious to deny that any serious diminishment of reading skills has followed the relaxation of traditional authority and control. Those on the right, by contrast, have been equally concerned to show that permissiveness in this area as elsewhere in our society has had harmful consequences. But there is no doubt that, whatever the facts, if there are any, it is widely perceived that illiteracy is spreading and that it is a most serious matter. A 1989 Carnegie Foundation survey found that 64 percent of college and university professors believed that "too many students ill-suited to academic life are now enrolling in colleges and universities." In the social world, if not in the natural world, what is perceived to be the fact is at least as important as what may objectively be the fact. Illiteracy has stood high on the social agenda in recent years, and it has been widely accepted that the matter is so serious that as Jonathan Kozol, who has made himself into a national spokesman for the cause of combating illiteracy, says simply, "The nation is at risk." Numerous reports have been written by prestigious foundations, tax-exempt research institutes set up, campaigns started headed by such distinguished public figures as Harold McGraw, funds appropriated, programs begun in the schools and elsewhere.

As a print-based institution, literature was bound to be deeply affected by any change in the status of print and the writing-reading skills needed to use it. In the long run the shift, which is at the center of the transformation to postindustrialism, from a book to an electronic culture, of which the literacy crisis is one major symptom, marks the end of the old literature. But in the short run, the effects, though serious, have not looked quite so catastrophic. Most immediately, the literacy crisis, whether imagined or factual, has brought about the conversion, discussed in chapter 3, of the English departments in most American universities from the teaching of literature to the teaching of writing and reading skills. More obliquely, and much less obviously, the literacy crisis, though studiously ignored, has been the social setting for the advanced criticism of recent years which has busied itself on a philosophical level with the same questions about literacy, readers, reading, and interpretation that are so disturbing the larger society.

Harold Bloom has told us of writer-readers who must by means of misprision creatively misread earlier texts to avoid being influenced by and sounding like their predecessors. Reading badly is, paradoxically, reading well in the Bloomian literary scene. Structuralists have argued for "writerly" over "readerly" texts—that is, books in which readers determine the meanings by their own interests rather than subjecting themselves, in the way literate people once did, to an "authoritarian" text that controls and limits meaning. Various phenomenological "reader-response" and "reception aesthetic" types of literary criticism have described texts as incomplete and filled with gaps, making reading a "problematic" activity, not an exact skill, and calling for a multiplicity of interpretations, no one of which is right or "privileged" over any other.

Interpretation, a very subjective activity, has replaced reading and understanding. The extreme democratic view, in which anyone's reading of a text is as true as any other, is legitimated by hermeneutics, a general theory of interpretation that posits that meaning is never in the text but always in the theory of interpretation applied to it. Deconstruction, the most radical of the modern literary theories, assumes a basic indeterminacy in all language and a consequent uncertainty of meaning in any text, making reading always relative and problematic. At the extreme of this kind of criticism where deconstruction resides, there isn't finally anything there to read, only tracks and traces, and an infinite regression of deferred realities, each giving a momentary illusion of substance to the other, but eventuating in emptiness. We can sum up this reader-centered criticism by saying that the concept of the *book*—ordered, controlled, teleological, referential, and autonomously meaningful—to be *read* by literate readers has been replaced by the *text*, fragmented, contradictory, incomplete, relativistic, arbitrary, and indeterminate, to be *interpreted* by people who have a great deal of difficulty piecing out the broken signs on the printed page.

At this elevated level of philosophical discussion, there is, of course, no thought of or concern for illiteracy in any schoolroom sense. Bloom's "misprision" is an epistemological not an educational issue. Criticism has wanted and acknowledged no relationship between its own sophisticated intellectual activities and the grungy business of adults who can't read enough to fill out welfare forms, or indulged children squatting for hours before the television rather than reading books. But looking back on the late twentieth century, social historians surely will not be able to avoid noticing and correlating the simultaneous appearance of electronic media that make reading less interesting and necessary, declines in literacy, the disappearance of a book-based literature, and, if the analysis bothers to go this far down, the development of a radical type of literary criticism that problematized the central literary activities of reading and writing, which had previously been assumed to be free of impediment.

In this broad view of historical change, what might, not altogether jokingly, be styled the "poetics of illiteracy," has performed, in a rather remarkable way, the standard institutional function of literary criticism. When the scene is limited to the literary world alone, deconstruction and the activist social criticisms that have succeeded it, feminism and Marxism, appear like destroying angels, seeking the death of literature by showing that it doesn't exist, that its putative poets don't write it, that its language is meaningless, that it has in the past only been the instrument of masculine attempts to dominate the female or of capitalism's exploitation of the masses. But in the wider scene of the electronic revolution as a whole, in which literature is only one small part, reader-centered criticism appears as a secondary form of legitimation, functioning in the usual way of this kind of institutional activity, to meet and explain away, or deal with in some fashion, dangers to literature. In the threatening circumstances of steadily increasing illiteracy, criticism accepted the facts, and explained them in a very sophisticated way that accommodated literature to, rather than letting it simply be overwhelmed by, the new circumstances. "Books are hard to read," the advanced criticism said in effect, "and often boring, and people nowadays have trouble in reading them. But the difficulty lies in the nature of language itself and of writing, and therefore no one is to be blamed for the difficulties experienced in reading texts since that is the normal situation. Where 'the problematics of reading' were previously concealed, literature will now openly acknowledge them, and even show how to maximize the situation." Having cleared the ground, tacitly accepting the fact that from now on reading literature, or anything else, is going to be a much less rigorous business, producing much looser understandings, the advanced criticism proceeded to make the difficulty of reading into a virtue rather than a defect, proposing that a loose and relativistic understanding of what it means to read can be really quite advantageous, offering opportunities for freedom, individuality, and creativity for everyone, all highly prized qualities in modern democratic society.

In this way, positing an open text, a free activity of interpretation, and a relativistic understanding of the ways in which meaning is made in the world, the advanced criticism adapted literature to the waning of the Gutenberg age by building the difficulties of reading into it. It went even farther and claimed a privileged position for literature in these circumstances as a type of discourse endlessly self-conscious about the problematics of reading, interpretation, and making meaning, frequently making these very questions its central subject.

Whether deconstruction has saved literature remains in doubt, but it seems unlikely. Literature remained and remains printed texts, complex and wordy, while in the larger social world electronics have already become the primary means of communication. Not only has television displaced the printed book with what are perceived as more attractive and effective forms of information, but it increasingly defines what constitutes information and understanding. Among the electronic information and communication technologies, television has most obviously and deeply disturbed existing society and affected conscious-ness. It is not a bad idea to seek explanations for any change in present society in the television—*cherchez la télé*. The computer might almost be treated as an advanced form of writing and printing, but television is an openly revolutionary force, pictorial rather than verbal, vigorously at work everywhere in the world, changing all it touches, politics, news, religion, sports, "life-styles," and consumption. Such common culture as we still have comes largely from television. Its power in relation to the codex book was nicely demonstrated in a recent event involving a series of public television interviews in 1988 between the television newsman and commentator Bill Moyers and the mythogra-pher Joseph Campbell, now deceased. Their subject was the mystical views about primal myths, a typical romantic print-society subject, that Campbell had expressed in books like *The Hero with a Thousand Faces*. This book printed years earlier by Princeton University Press had, because of its sensational subject matter—spiritual and Jung-ian—and its publication in the fashionable Bollingen series, sold well for a university press book. Lifetime sales of the average scholarly monograph had by 1988 fallen below a thousand copies, almost en-tirely to libraries, and the Campbell book had always done better than this. But after the Moyers interviews, *The Hero with a Thousand Faces* sold approximately 35,000 copies a month for the first few months, and Princeton University Press was soon proudly advertising that it had sold over 200,000 copies in one year. The lesson is clear. If you want people to read, or at least buy, a book, nowadays, advertise it on television!

The problem for literature in all this is not just that interest in reading great books is diminishing as television watching increases, or even that reading of all kinds is becoming a lost skill in a time when more and more information is available on the electronic screen. At the deepest level the worldview of television is fundamentally at odds with the worldview of a literature based on the printed book. As television watching increases, therefore, and more and more people derive, quite unconsciously, their sense of reality and their existential situation in it from television, the assumptions about the world that have been identified with literature will become less and less plausible, and in time will become downright incredible. By way of an obvious example we can take the role of the author. Literature and the book feature an author—someone thinks them up, organizes the ideas, and writes them. The author has been a major figure in literature, the person who knows something and writes it, but television, like the moving picture earlier, demotes authors to script writers, or treatment editors, and buries them, even more than films, among a host of other production credits in which only the star-actor and much less frequently the producer and the director stand out. In fifty years television has not made a single author famous.

The author is not the only character whose situation is rearranged and personality redefined by the transition from a book to a television world. The audience undergoes an equally radical though different kind of shift. Marshall McLuhan thought that television would return people from the isolation and inwardness of modern life and its characteristic informational mode, reading, to what he styled "the global village," where everyone shared the same jolly interests and participated simultaneously in the common business of the community, whether games or soaps or politics. The "tiny screen" does often strive for this interactive effect by involving studio audiences with the folksy performers, and news programs have an odd effect not unlike small town gossip on a cosmic scale, "Have you heard about the latest shelling in Beirut?"—"Isn't the flood in Bangladesh terrible!" But, while there may be some illusion of participation—"You are there at the tearing down of the Berlin Wall"—television viewers do not interact with others as they would in a localized oral situation of the small town or village. Their situation as viewers reenacts the isolation of the members of "the lonely crowd," the mass society of the urbanized

West, passive consumers being manipulated by those who control their sense of the world. As many as 150 million people are said to have at one time or another, in America alone, simultaneously watched a particular sporting event, such as baseball's World Series, or a public occasion like the funeral of President Kennedy, or even the showing of a popular movie like one of the James Bond spy thrillers. But amid this vast multitude, each individual sits mostly alone, usually in the dark, watching quietly the staged images of the world, interspersed with advertisements, flickering on the small screen. The reader as defined by literature and print was perhaps even more locked in solipsism, but he or she was intensely active mentally, rather than passive, trying to decode the complex words and the intricate structures of printed reality in order to get at a transcendent truth on the other side of the printed page.

Words are the essential stuff of literature, but visual images are the building blocks of television, which is, by way of one example, the reason why the classical theater, which has been a theater of words, loses so much, almost everything in cases like Shakespeare, in adaptations for television. There is language on television in the form of speech and occasional printed material, but the continued poor quality of speakers in TV sets offers an insight into how little concern the medium has with words. The pictures on the tube are constantly improved, but the speakers remain rudimentary. Visual images don't provide the same kind of truth as words. What they say is not necessarily inferior but it is different. Meaning is much more on the surface, experienced immediately rather than discovered by extended in-depth analysis of the image. The meaning of the visual image is also far less complex, lacking the multiplicity of meanings characteristic of single words and the ironic ambivalence set up between words.

These differences in verbal and visual epistemology extend beyond the single word and image to the larger organizational structures. Television is a nervous, continuous collage, always ramshackle, never put together with much care, quickly used and soon discarded. The *esprit de système* and the fixity so characteristic of printing and carried over into the craft emphasis of literature and its idealization of iconicity have no place in television, which produces not classics but entertainment consumables that seldom have any existence beyond their brief moment on the screen. Where language in the printed book tends toward the intricacies of paragraph and chapter, elaborate themes and form, the images of television are characteristically episodic, brief, and ephemeral. Where the book is intended to be read and reread, opening increased depths of meaning on each reading, the television spectacle is seen once in a flash and then, except for occasional reruns, gone forever. The truth of television images is not engraved in stone but is provisional, contemporary, transitory. Those who work in TV are quite aware that their medium does not favor complex meanings, and they adjust their material accordingly. Story and plot are minimal or nonexistent. Individual images, not continuity, are what matters, and they come in such rapid succession and last such a brief time—the famous fifteen-second byte—that it is difficult, and unnecessary, to see any cause-and-effect pattern developing. Frequent advertising interruptions in American commercial television, and the standard thirty-minute or sixty-minute time slot further prevent anything more than the most conventional story patterns from being used.

Intricacy of structure, complexity of meaning, irony, ambiguity, multivalency, indeterminacy—the secondary characteristics of print— were extrapolated by the old book culture. Densely woven poems like *The Waste Land* or "Thirteen Ways of Looking at a Blackbird," novels that have mystery at their center like *The Trial* and *Heart of Darkness*, plays that take the complexities of illusion and reality for their subjects like *Six Characters in Search of an Author* and *Rosencrantz and Guildenstern Are Dead*—these were the enduring classics of modern literature, embodying, it was believed, permanent human truths, written by authors of imaginative genius, capable of sustaining endless subtle interpretations by scholars and critics.

Looking backward it can be seen that literature and print both embodied in their related ways the assumptions of an earlier humanism about such matters as truth, imagination, language, and history. Television, however, is not just a new way of doing old things but a radically different way of seeing and interpreting the world. Visual images not words, simple open meanings not complex and hidden, transience not permanence, episodes not structures, theater not truth. Literature's ability to coexist with television, which many take for granted, seems less likely when we consider that as readers turn into viewers, as the skill of reading diminishes, and as the world as seen through a television screen feels and looks more pictorial and immediate, belief in a word-based literature will inevitably diminish.

7

The Battle for the Word:

Dictionaries, Deconstructors,

and Language Engineers

Samuel Johnson's great dictionary of the English language was finished in 1755, nine years after work began with an optimistic estimate that it would be finished in three years. But given Johnson's irregular work habits and the unexpected difficulty of the task, the work dragged and schedules broke down. His own words in the Preface to the *Dictionary* convey feelingly Johnson's near panic when he came face to face with the reality of language and realized the difficulty of what he had to do:

> Consider that no dictionary of a living tongue ever can be perfect, since, while it is hastening to publication, some words are budding, and some falling away; that a whole life cannot be spent upon syntax and etymology, and that even a whole life would not be sufficient; that he, whose design includes whatever language can express, must often speak of what he does not understand; that a writer will sometimes be hurried by eagerness to the end, and sometimes faint with weariness under a task, which Scaliger compares to the labours of the anvil and the mine; that what is obvious is not always known, and what is known is not always present; that

sudden fits of inadvertency will surprise vigilance, slight avocations will seduce attention, and casual eclipses of the mind will darken learning; and that the writer shall often in vain trace his memory, at the moment of need, for that which yesterday he knew with intuitive readiness, and which will come uncalled in his thoughts tomorrow.

No wonder the first volume was not completed until 1753, seven years after work had begun, and the second only in 1755, at which time the bookseller Andrew Millar, who was coordinating the project, could say, according to Boswell, on the receiving the final sheets of copy, "Thank GOD I have done with *him*." To which a deflated Johnson could only reply, "I am glad . . . that he thanks GOD for anything."

But at last it was finished. About 40,000 entries, 116,000 illustrative quotations, over 2,500 double-column pages, a preface, history of the language, and description of English grammar, all sumptuously printed in 2,000 copies of two large folios each, priced at £4 10s. Once the work was accomplished, the "humble drudge" became "Dictionary Johnson," and his book became the English language, ordered word by word alphabetically, and numerically page by page, each entry locked in place by a standard format—spelling, pronunciation, etymology, series of definitions—each meaning established by quotations from the best English writers.

So solidly, objectively real is the dictionary that this, we still feel, *is* the English language, yet Johnson himself reveals in his famous "Preface" that in all its parts, lexicon, pronunciation, spelling, etymologies, and above all meanings, his dictionary was an arbitrary selection from and ordering of what he in the course of assembling the dictionary had come to see as the baseless and unsystematic babbling of imperfect people that he called "the boundless chaos of a living speech." The drudgery of day-by-day assembling the entries of the dictionary gradually taught Johnson that language is no more a product of logic than it is a catalog of the world. It belongs, he learned painfully, to history and the vagaries of human existence, to a world where "vanity affects peculiar pronunciations and meanings," where the diction of laborers and merchants is "casual and mutable . . . formed for some temporary or local convenience." Advanced societies, he discovered, have the leisure to increase knowledge and to produce new words; fashion and convenience create terms which flourish briefly and then die easily; science amplifies language "with words deflected from their original sense." These are only the beginning of the linguistic accidents that cause endless problems for the lexicographer:

> The tropes of poetry will make hourly encroachments, and the metaphorical will become the current sense: pronunciation will be varied by levity or ignorance, and the pen must at length comply with the tongue; illiterate writers will, at one time or another, by publick infatuation, rise into renown, who, not knowing the original import of words, will use them with colloquial licentiousness, confound distinction, and forget propriety. As politeness increases, some expressions will be considered as too gross and vulgar for the delicate, others as too formal and ceremonious for the gay and airy; new phrases are, therefore, adopted, which must, for the same reasons, be in time dismissed.

Traces of linguistic essentialism remain embedded in much of Johnson's phrasing, for example, "the original import of words." But Johnson had found in the course of working on the dictionary that language is not "Adamic" in the sense of that term that Hans Aarsleff has used to describe the type of theories that posit some linguistic essence in language, some absolute connection between words and things, or words and ideas. "And out of the ground the Lord God formed every beast of the field, and every fowl of the air, and brought them unto Adam, to see what he would call them: and whatsoever Adam called every living creature, that *was* the name thereof." Language, Johnson discovered, was social. Words and their meanings, as well as grammar, do not refer to some prior external reality, are not fixed in some permanent way in and of themselves, but are always changing—"the boundless chaos of a living speech"—to suit the needs and interests of those who use them.

Any attempt to order in a dictionary words that slide and slither about in this way came soon to seem mere folly to Johnson: "To enchain syllables and to lash the wind, are equally the undertakings of pride, unwilling to measure its desires by its strength." Some principle of "constancy and stability" was needed, however, to move ahead with the dictionary project, entry by entry, day by day, and so Johnson, a professional writer in the print-based literary system, working for printers to produce a printed book that made a systematic language out of random words, inevitably found it, or rather made the required organizational principle, by deciding that printed books provided the authority for "true" words. A word was real enough to be included in his dictionary only if it had appeared in print. He omitted many familiar words because, he said, "I had never read them."

Print also provided the authority for meanings. Recognizing that most words had at least several meanings, as well as an infinity of shadings, and that these changed over time, Johnson recorded a variety of definitions for many words, though not in historical order of appearance. That refinement awaited the appearance of the *New English Dictionary on Historical Principles* in the late nineteenth century. Johnson accepted a particular sense of a word as authentic only if it was supported by a passage in a printed book, which was then excerpted and printed under the appropriate entry. But not all books, and not even all passages in the chosen works, were acceptable as the authority for the existence of words and their meanings. Johnson excluded books whose authors or subjects he considered immoral, and as Robert DeMaria has recently shown by reading the complete dictionary and analyzing some of its critical entries in great detail, he gave the dictionary "an important moral message . . . chiefly by presenting quotations that, besides illustrating the meanings of words, teach fundamental points of morality." DeMaria after going through the 116,000 illustrative quotations concludes that the point of the way that the dictionary was assembled is finally, in Johnson's own words, "to shew that the end of learning is piety." To which we might add that the point of his methodology is that the printed word is alone the true word and that the meaning of words is established by the best writers in a language.

There were also practical considerations of how much he could read, and he narrowed the books from which he drew his words to what he called, echoing Spenser speaking of Chaucer, "the wells of English undefiled," the books printed between 1580 and 1660, between Sidney's works and those of the Restoration. It would be impossible to check whether he did limit himself to these books; I suspect he did not. Certainly his illustrations of meanings were taken from the writings of his own age more often than not. John Locke is quoted more than any other author.

It all looks like a straightforward, though difficult, piece of bookmaking, a brilliant pragmatic solution by a professional writer to a set of practical problems. But famous events that took place at the time of the publication of the dictionary reveal that dictionary making is deeply involved in a continuing social struggle for linguistic power. Because language is not fixed but endlessly plastic, it lies open to manipulation, and whoever can control language has an instrument of enormous power in their hands, or, better, their mouths. This power derives from normative assumptions about language. Most people take a commonsensical view of language, assuming that it refers with some precision to an actual world and to our ideas. Language itself is usually no more suspect but is thought of as an objective reality consisting of so many words with definite meanings—the lexicon—capable of being assembled in larger units in correct and truthful ways, in accordance with the rules of grammar. In other words, language is there; it exists in itself, and it names the world. As a result of this commonsense trust in the language and its truth, those who can shape language can determine what is reality and what is truth. A dictionary is one of the primary means of claiming and exercising this kind of linguistic power.

Feminists have given us convincing examples of the way that language can control truth in the "masculinizing" of language—"he" and "him" for "everyone," or "man" for "people." These and similar usages have factualized male importance, making it seem, because embedded in language, given and natural that men rather than women do and are everything. One of the big revolutionary first moves in the linguistic power game is to demonstrate, as Johnson did in his preface and as deconstructive theories have done in our time, the arbitrary and insubstantial nature of the received standard language. This clears out the old controls over language and makes room for linguistic revolutionaries to declare their own authority over the word. Once in place, the new linguistic authority establishes itself by making it seem in various ways that it is *the* true language, with unchanging rules and fixed meanings grounded in some reality outside itself. The Académie française with its legal power to say what is and what is not *le vrai français* offers the most obvious institutionalization of linguistic control. Dictionaries have been one of the principal instruments in modern linguistic power struggles, and Johnson's dictionary played an important part in the eighteenth-century struggle in which middle-class professionals were wresting cultural and political as well as linguistic power from the old aristocracy. The dynamics of that battle for verbal power were revealed in Johnson's famous quarrel with Lord Chesterfield.

In many ways, Philip Stanhope, fourth earl of Chesterfield, was a perfect image of the old oral order that was giving way to print during the eighteenth century. He was a brilliant conversationalist and notable public speaker—which Johnson for all his fluency in talk was not—famous for his eloquent orations in the House of Lords and for his letters, which he did not, of course, deign to print. In all ways he was the *beau idéal* of the ancien régime and of polite letters, an aristocratic amateur who wrote in an elegant fashion for the amusement and instruction of a small circle of friends of similar taste. The term "the King's English" had been coined by Shakespeare about 1598— "Abusing God's patience and the King's English"—and Chesterfield was its *arbiter elegantiarum* who defended the old right, asserted by the term, the King's English, of the aristocracy to determine polite usage. As such Chesterfield was the appropriate person to serve as the patron of the *Dictionary*, and Johnson had in 1746 been persuaded, reluctantly, by the booksellers who financed his dictionary to address in the required fulsome style a proposal advertising the dictionary to the noble earl.

Chesterfield accepted the homage as his proper due, and gave Johnson £10, but in the years between then and the completion of the work, he expressed no further interest and gave no help. In 1754, when the *Dictionary* was about to appear, however, Chesterfield, hearing rumors of its probable success, was willing once more to play the patron in order to gratify his noted vanity and to reassert the claim implicit in the patronage system that letters derived their authority and language its standards from the manners, tastes, and values of the ruling class. And so he smoothly gave the work his imprimatur, making, he said, with a glance at Roman history, and a bemused democratic gesture, "a total surrender of all my rights and privileges in the English language, as a free-born British subject, to the said Mr. Johnson, during the term of his dictatorship."

He went on to offer some advice to the dictionary maker of a kind that shows pretty clearly how and why his class was linguistically and politically losing ground. Johnson should not, he cautioned him, forget that the word *flirtation* was the *mot* of a lady of fashion to whom Chesterfield gallantly referred as "the most beautiful mouth in the world." Nor should he fail to define the obscure verb *to fuzz* as meaning "dealing twice together with the same pair of cards, for luck." Above all, the lexicographer should insist on the necessity of restricting the much overworked word *vastly*, as in the description of a snuffbox as "vastly pretty, because it was vastly little." Needless to say, Johnson included none of this verbal fluff in a sober middle-class dictionary designed "to shew that the end of learning is piety."

Johnson's response to this kind of patronizing, the famous "Letter to Lord Chesterfield," expressed the views of a professional writer who earned his living using words to supply the public with what it would pay to read. The letter still stands as the magna carta of the modern author, the announcement that the days of courtly letters are ended, that authors are the true source of their work, that the writer is no longer dependent on the patron or on the hierarchical social system the aristocrat represents. Language now belongs to the professional writers. "Seven years, my Lord, have now past, since I waited in your outward rooms, or was repulsed from your door; during which time I have been pushing on my work through difficulties, of which it is useless to complain, and brought it at last, to the verge of publication, without one act of assistance, one word of encouragement, or one smile of favour." He clinched the matter by publishing the *Dictionary* without a dedication and without a reference to the man he now openly declared to be not "a lord among wits; but . . . only a wit among lords." The English language, the quarrel with Chesterfield established, was defined and controlled by professional writers like Samuel Johnson, whose name alone appeared on the title page, and the many others whose general authority over language was established by the 116,000 quotations in the *Dictionary* from their works validating the existence and the meaning of words.

Johnson's dictionary and its assumptions about the ownership of language were very much in the cultural mainstream. From the time of its appearance until the middle of the present century, it was generally taken for granted by a print society that language is ruled by its professional writers, particularly its major literary figures, who make language their chief study, maintain its strength, expand the range of possibilities, create new words and meanings, rework the tropes, and in the end are the ultimate authorities on wordcraft. Without laboring the obvious, what have modern writers and critics talked about except language! Johnson's contemporary Condillac, in his *Essai sur l'origine des connoissances humaines* (1746), which Johnson may have known, had conceded that "of all writers, it is in the poets that the genius of language finds most vivid expression," and during the course of the nineteenth century the imaginative or creative writers of literature, as the poets came to be called, continued to build up a special relationship to language. By the time of his *Defense of Poetry* (1821), Shelley could claim that the poets had actually created language and kept it alive: "Language is vitally metaphorical; that is, it marks the before unapprehended relations of things and perpetuates their apprehension, until the words which represent them become, through time, signs for portions or classes of thoughts instead of pictures of integral thoughts; and then if no new poets should arise to create afresh the associations which have been thus disorganized, language will be dead to all the nobler purposes of human intercourse. . . . language itself is poetry."

This literary identification with language carried on into Valéry's twentieth-century fiat, "Literature is, and can be nothing other than, a kind of extension and application of certain properties of language." And as late as 1945, T. S. Eliot in "The Social Function of Poetry" could still treat the special responsibility of the writer for language as a recognized part of the social order: "We may say, then, that just as the first duty of a man *qua* citizen is to his country, so his first duty *qua* poet is to the language of his country. First, he has the duty to *preserve* that language: his use of it must not weaken, coarsen, or degrade it. Second, he has the duty to *develop* that language, to bring it up to date, to investigate its unexplored possibilities. So far as he expresses, in his poetry, what other people feel, he is also affecting that feeling by making it more conscious: in giving people words for their feelings, he is teaching them something about themselves." Eliot's contemporary Ezra Pound put it more simply. For him, poetry was simply "language charged with meaning to the utmost possible degree." The general acceptance of such views is testified to in a humble way by the many calls and letters that still come to university English departments asking for authoritative judgment on some pedantic matter of spelling or grammar, often to settle a bet, as if English professors by virtue of their connection to writing and writers had some special linguistic authority.

From the earliest days of Western society, writers have associated their art with the uncommonly skillful management of the common language—Virgil and his line a day, the unpolished *Aeneid* ordered destroyed on his deathbed. In the high romantic period, literary language was still often thought of as only an intensified version of ordinary speech, what Wordsworth called "the real language of men in a state of vivid sensation." But in the modern period, literary language has increasingly been treated as a privileged tongue escaping the limitations of ordinary language, which is viewed as flawed by its employment in the business of the world. For Flaubert in *Madame Bovary la parole humaine* is a "cracked cauldron on which we beat out melodies," and Conrad's "Teacher of Languages" in *Under Western Eyes* speaks of words as "the foes of reality." Joyce's fictional poet, Stephen Dedalus, in *Portrait of the Artist as a Young Man* calls language one of the nets, along with religion, family, and nation, flung over the soul of the artist to destroy him. These and other writers since their time have assumed it to be the special mission of literature to refine and improve the inadequacies of the "speech of the tribe" by finding Flaubert's *les mots justes*, or creating like Joyce in *Finnegans Wake* a new highly charged language from the broken fragments of the old.

These new languages have been among the most spectacular and interesting achievements of modern literature. In addition to neologists like Joyce, there have been many creators of many various specialized literary creoles, writers of nonsense languages like Lewis Carroll, Orphics like Nabokov, verbal reprocessors like E. E. Cummings, hermeticists like Wallace Stevens, all of whom conceived of literature as a new artificial language more trustworthy and powerful than the social languages of the given world:

> Then we
> As we beheld her striding there alone,
> Knew that there never was a world for her
> Except the one she sang and, singing, made.

As this century has proceeded, negative attitudes toward language of all kinds have increasingly prevailed, and writers began what George Steiner, the historian of "the language of silence," has called a "retreat from the word." In the face of what was felt to be an increasingly incoherent Babel in the public world, "pidgin, not pentecost," as Steiner puts it, writers have responded by trying to avoid the humbug, cant, and jargon of the world by saying less and less. Increasing amounts of silence and a minimization of words were for Hemingway, Beckett, Kafka, William Carlos Williams, Pinter, Larkin, and many others the only honest speech still available, and they deliberately reduced the language of literature to the barest and plainest terms, distrusting larger and grander statements as empty and likely to break down in the face of actuality. A writer like William Faulkner, no less uneasy with words, played a variation on this linguistic pessimism not by retreating to minimalism but by treating language as so untrustworthy that it is necessary to pile it higher and higher in the hope of catching by chance somewhere and sometime the needle of meaning in the haystack of words and phrases.

In time, the sound and fury signifying almost nothing of Faulkner's novels and the near silence—"qua, qua, qua"—of Beckett's almost empty stages were backed up by a linguistic theory that systematized literary doubts about language and reinforced in a new fashion literature's linguistic privilege. In the latter nineteenth century, literature, at least in the academies, had been nearly absorbed, subjected really, as we have seen earlier in connection with the admission of the subject to the Oxford honors school, by the historical study of Indo-European philology. Literature in this language theory was nothing more than a historical record of linguistic change. But the twentieth century brought a number of new major theories of language more compatible with romantic and modern literary interests than vowel shifts and laws governing sound changes from one language to another. Saussure's structuralist linguistics appeared early in the century in Geneva; the analytical or ordinary language schools developed at Oxford and Cambridge around such distinguished names as Russell, Wittgenstein, Austin, and Ayer; the anthropological school concentrating on American Indian languages emerged in the work of figures like Edward Sapir and Benjamin Whorf; while the generative-grammar theory of Noam Chomsky posited an innate universal grammar. Parallel to these philosophies of language, a scientific linguistics grew up—phonetics, morphology, semantics, sociolinguistics, psycholinguistics, and many other specialties, offering such groups as the Prague linguistic school precise ways of describing what literature does with words. All these linguistic theories offered literature new opportunities to support its claim to a special relation to language. All have been employed to that end to a greater or lesser degree, but it has been Saussure's structural linguistics that, particularly after the 1960s, has provided a basis for explaining the special nature of literary language and a philosophical setting for literature in all of its aspects.

Structuralism systematizes traditional literary doubts about language by positing a radically isolated linguistic situation. Language no longer goes out to and names the world as Adam named the animals. There is no essential connection between the verbal sign and the signified. The word does not record the historical development of an ur-language, proto–Indo-European, into numerous individual languages in accordance with laws of phonetic change. Nor is it the speech of actual people in actual circumstances, for this is only the noise of the world, the *paroles* of day-to-day life. Language, as Saussure described it, derives from neither things nor history nor living people. It is an arbitrary and abstract system for generating meaning. The system, *la langue*, is sufficient unto itself, independent of the world of things and indifferent to the passage of time. It defines the world, of course, pointing to this or that, and it has a history of successive paradigms, but it makes these conditions rather than being made by them. At its most basic level, the system turns on the relation of a few sounds—approximately forty in English—the phonemes, arbitrarily chosen out of the infinite range of sounds made by human beings. Sounds not included in this set have no meaning, if they are heard at all they are merely "noise." The significant phonemes could be fewer or more numerous without affecting the basic language system, for they have no innate meaning or connection with what they signify. Their meaning is established not by referentiality or historicity of any kind but by their place in the system, by difference from other sounds in the language system: "p" is nothing in itself, only not "t." As with the sounds, so with the words and sentences and texts built up out of the sounds in conformity with a set of rules, *la langue*, that governs the meaningful use of the pieces in the set, as the rules of a game prescribe the moves that are meaningful in the course of a game. One of the most common moves in the language meaning game is, for example, to set up a binary opposition, subject and object, or poetry and prose.

The phonemic theory that provides the foundation for this contemporary view of language was not available to Samuel Johnson when he was constructing his dictionary, but he grasped the central idea at the level of the word and spoke in his preface of the necessity "that the explanation, and the word explained, should be always reciprocal."

This meant explanations that were "unavoidably reciprocal or circular, as *hind,* the *female of the stag; stag, the male of the hind:* sometimes easier words are changed into harder, as *burial* into *sepulture* or *interment, drier* into *desiccative, dryness* into *siccity* or *aridity, fit* into *paroxysm:* for the easiest word, whatever it be, can never be translated into one more easy."

Structuralism, though organized around speech, assumes language in the way that it is experienced in the reading, not the talking, situation. Sounds are cut off from the sensory world and removed from historical change. Words and sentences, made up of bits of sound that refer to nothing, have their meaning not in some positive quality but merely in their difference from other words and sentences, which also lack positive qualities. Absence rather than presence is the inescapable condition of language. The reality of words is an enfeebled and wobbly condition expressed in structuralist and poststructuralist linguistic terms like *trace, supplement, deferral, indeterminacy,* and *polyvalency.* Neither the human speakers, writers, nor listeners who live within the language system control it. They merely tend a system that, like some vast computer, turns out meanings and interpretations according to the rules that have been handed down to them. Only the system, *la langue,* the software program of the language game for making meaning, is real, and the infinity of individual utterances produced according to its rules are only Yeats's "spume that plays upon a ghostly paradigm."

An arbitrary system is the central reality in structural linguistics, and the world it posits is narrow. Not solipsistic, but close to it. Nothing has any meaning or being in its own right, but, cut off from all else, derives the only being and meaning it can have from its location in an arbitrary structure. By the late 1960s, darker forms of structuralism, known as poststructuralism or deconstruction, further deepened literary pessimism about language by calling attention to the incomplete, inadequate, contradictory, and flawed nature of all forms of discourse. All texts in this view are a sham, a mere pretense of a meaning that will not stand up to close reading. (*Reading* is always the given condition, speech being treated as only a special instance of writing.) The difficulties lie not in some careless use of but are indigenous to language.

Paul de Man's noted essay "Semiology and Rhetoric" (1979) provides a model of the way deconstructive reading proceeds. Language, following Charles Sanders Peirce, is defined as "pure rhetoric" in which the reading of each word or sign does not lead to "closure" in some truth or some fact but only to another word or sign in an endless process of *différence*, by which "one sign gives birth to another." Each word or concept, that is to say, does not terminate in some solid reality but endlessly requires explanation by another word or concept, which in turn requires further words and concepts. Grammar and logic give an illusion of a structured, unproblematic meaning, but close analysis always reveals "vertiginous possibilities of referential aberration." Interpretation leads always not to clarity but to "greater complications." The existence of the "literal meaning . . . is denied by the figurative meaning." Two plausible readings of the same passage "engage each other in direct confrontation, for the one reading is precisely the error denounced by the other and has to be undone by it." Grammar and rhetoric are assumed to work in the same direction, supporting one another, but on close inspection, "rhetoric radically suspends logic," leaving the two main principles of linguistic structuration not in ironic relationship but at fundamental odds.

For all its iconoclasm, deconstruction, though it radicalizes continues to embody many traditional conceptions about literature. It assumes, for example, that the reading situation on which literature is based is the epistemological norm, and it carries the traditional modern hostility of literature toward public language to its nihilistic extreme. Deconstruction also continues to privilege the forms of literature. Where other forms of discourse create illusions of absolute, final, essential meanings, "totalization" or the "metaphysics of presence," offering as real "the concepts of causality, of the subject, of identity, of referential and revealed truth," literature alone remains self-consciously skeptical of its own words and concepts. Literature is in this understanding "the most advanced and refined model of deconstruction." Only "the literary text simultaneously asserts and denies the authority of its own rhetorical mode," simultaneously offering instances of the way in which words are used to create "truth" and accepting the impossibility of truth in any final sense. As de Man sums it up, "Literature as well as criticism—the difference between them being delusive—is condemned (or privileged) to be forever the most rigorous and, consequently, the most unreliable language in terms of which man names and modifies himself."

No wonder that Gerald Graff (1989) after surveying de Man's work remarks that, for all of their seeming strangeness, structuralism and deconstruction look remarkably like the latest attempt in a long historical line to establish the importance of literature by discrediting ordinary language and attributing extraordinary powers to literary language:

> The states of interpretive catastrophe cultivated by de Man are rooted less in some universal need to control our discourse than in de Man's need to associate literature with "vertiginous possibilities of referential aberration." To those of a certain generation, who were taught in college that the upstaging of practical, scientific, constative discourse is the special and privileged business of literature, de Man's theory and practice will not seem so unfamiliar or radical. They are a throwback to the old opposition between literature and "statement," by which literature has long been seen as an alternative to the technocratic way of knowing, a consolation prize for letting others run the world.

It is necessary only to add that in de Man's case, as in that of many other structuralists and deconstructionists, these philosophies have been the instruments of a fierce political will to attack and discredit those who have long been running the world. Intellectuals are less and less satisfied with the social and economic booby prize.

But for all its passive aggressiveness, the more radical criticisms of our time have created a dreary linguistic scene. Locked forever in the library reading a book, we are solemnly assured that "there is nothing outside the text" and nothing very much inside it either in texts where "the absence of the transcendental signified extends the domain and the interplay of signification *ad infinitum*" (Derrida). But deconstructive views of language can become fun when we turn away from the academy to a more public scene where two worldly politicians, Ron Ziegler and John Ehrlichman, in the course of the Watergate scandal, when confronted with proof that earlier White House statements had been lies, instantly and extemporaneously declared that those earlier statements were "no longer operative." There is something brilliant about this applied deconstruction, and though it would probably be an exaggeration to speak of the present as a Golden Age of Language, we do live in a time of extraordinary linguistic vitality, of confidence and power in the word, particularly the spoken word, which is totally at odds with deconstruction's and literature's view of words as evanescent and futile. Verbal energy in the modern world is unfortunately more often that of Ben Jonson's highly vocal alchemists, swindlers, whores, gluttons, lechers, projectors, and "cony catchers" than it is of Shakespeare's flashing wits and noble orators—"I have done the state some service, and they know't." But there is in our time the same quick ingenuity with words, indifference to formal rules, determination to make language serve human purposes, and the sense that words are intensely real and that you can do everything with them that mark the great characters of the Renaissance theater, Sir Epicure Mammon or King Lear.

Not the best of moral models, perhaps, but an expert, none greater, on how to use language, Adolf Hitler, tells us in a famous statement in *Mein Kampf* that "the power which has always started the greatest religious and political avalanches in history rolling has from time immemorial been the magic power of the spoken word, and that alone." And he was right. The world's words, some good, some terrible, contradictory, illogical, void, crackle with energy. Generals speak of "nuking villages back to the stone age" in order to save them, sportscasters tell it like it is, an electronic minister cries as he confesses to his sheep of having strayed from the path of righteousness, coaches inspire their players by assuring them that it's not over until it's over, youth gets it all together, name recognition ensures that people will get their calls answered. New "experts" in every field enhance their importance with specialized jargon like packaging, infrastructure, visibility generating machinery, high density population centers, media event, photo opportunity, and support industry peripherals. Policemen for some reason seem particularly fond of the kind of jargon that has them "apprehending perpetrators" and impounding "alleged suspect vehicles." It is a remarkable explosion of language, vulgar, crude, funny, ignorant, dangerous even, but clever, quick, alive, and effective. "We're the Pepsi Generation, Comin' at Ya, Goin' Strong." "Marlboro Country."

Most educated people wince with good reason at the jargon of blight and bloat that floods the media, for it is not just a matter of the old rules of grammar being broken, anarchy overtaking spelling, comma fault and dangling modifiers becoming brazen, and the jargons of a pompous dullness being amplified and broadcast with high-wattage sound equipment and even more powerful self-satisfaction throughout the land. The most inventive and powerful words heard in modern America are used in an openly immoral fashion, without, that is, any real concern for truth or logic or decency.

Not only do our fools coin words and turn phrases in a kind of national logorrhea, but our most skilled users of words, the "hidden persuaders," are unashamed and unrepentant verbal fudgers, exaggerators, if not outright liars, distorters, and cynical manipulators. Advertising copywriters associate a watery beer or a tinny car with sex and masculinity, slippery politicians promise what they have not the slightest intention of delivering—never heard of five minutes earlier— hired public relations specialists tell us that the latest chemical spill will not impact the environment, image makers pass off mediocrity for genius, Laputian technocrats who are in the loop bottomline the time frame, venal lawyers say the Brobdignagian "thing which is not." This new Babel purposely tries to sound like the down-to-earth words of the folks, but, as everyone knows who listens, the language that matters nowadays is made by modern language engineers, the public relations flacks, entertainers, media specialists, television personalities, advertising hypesters, bureaucrats, celebrity manufacturers and marketers, politicians and their image makers, technocrats, and singers of popular songs.

Descriptions of the modern science of manufacturing and marketing celebrities on the Pygmalion Principle tend to sound something like Jonathan Swift's *Modest Proposal*. You are not quite sure if your leg is being pulled when Irving J. Rein tells you in his book on making celebrities, *High Visibility*, that in the old days Lincoln became famous by freeing the slaves and Napoleon—complete with logo—by conquering Europe, but "today, most aspiring celebrities cannot count upon such circumstances." Fortunately our aspiring modern celebrities need not rely on the old-fashioned methods of Napoleon and Lincoln, for the modern media have the power to produce and broadcast images across the land, thereby creating "artificial fame." Fame is, however, really an out-of-date term. Celebrity, not fame, is achieved by using visibility-generating machinery to produce instant high visibility. Name recognition is what is wanted, and gotten, nowadays. People without talent or beauty or some other charismatic energy are advised not to despair, for people are finally more easily repackaged than other products. Beer when you get through with it is still beer, but cosmetic surgery, dentistry, wigs, dieting, exercise, speech lessons, psychological counseling, dress, being seen in the right place with the right people can make any old pig's ear into your silk purse. All that is needed is the desire to be a celebrity, and the money to pay for the "makeover," and you can become to your own trade what Lee Iacocca is to cars, Frank Perdue is to chickens, Carl Sagan is to astronomy, Truman Capote was to the art of the salon, and Arthur Schlesinger, Jr., is to history.

It sounds mad, but the transformation with images and words of "the ordinary into the visible, and the visible into the highly visible" works every day for business people, academics, actors, lawyers, doctors, politicians, and anyone else who wants to enter the bright celebrity world. It is easy to laugh, but the image makers are on to something of the utmost importance. As Rein and his colleagues put it, "Achievements are not achievements unless they are reported in the media." The media have the power to make things, including people, far more real, in the sense that they are intensely present to large numbers of the public, than older "reality making systems." You don't need to be famous to be a celebrity, but only if you become a celebrity will your fame be real. The actual events of your life, dull or exciting, have no reality in themselves, but an exciting "story line," which can speedily be created to order, can easily become real in the media.

We can all testify to the power of modern linguistic alchemy, for the public scene provides innumerable practical examples of its effectiveness in a time when politicians avoid the issue for the image, when public opinion polls establish the truth, and when the news is what appears on television. The situation has its tragic side in the successful propaganda of totalitarian states like Nazi Germany, North Korea, and Red China. But it has its lighter moments, too, such as the Watergate affair, when the world stood in amazement as John Mitchell, "the big Enchilada," and his cohorts, Colson, Magruder, Dean, Hunt, and others, used words as if they were silly putty to make it seem as if nothing had happened, and besides it was no one's responsibility. In H. R. Haldeman's "zero-defect system," where some people "stonewalled" it while others were "left to turn slowly in the wind," the active voice vanished into passive constructions, bribes became "increments in the form of currency," burglary "situation containment," and criminal conspiracy "the game plan."

In spite of literature's continuing shrill claims to "true" linguistic authority, the words that are heard and heeded in the land are nowadays the words of the people who have learned to use a new kind of public language, political in the sense of providing people with what they want, technological in the utilization of new methods of communication and information storage, economic in the sense of big payoffs for the ability to shape attitudes with words. Walter Lippmann, in his 1922 classic, *Public Opinion*, described the modern social conditions that have nourished this new alchemical language:

> The world that we have to deal with politically is out of reach, out of sight, out of mind. It has to be explored, reported, and imagined. Man is no Aristotelian god contemplating all existence at one glance. He is the creature of an evolution who can just about span a sufficient portion of reality to manage his survival, and snatch what on the scale of time are but a few moments of insight and happiness. . . . personal representation must be supplemented by representation of the unseen facts . . . [which] allow[s] us to escape from the intolerable and unworkable fiction that each of us must acquire a competent opinion about all public affairs.

Lippmann understood that the days when an individual could understand enough of the surrounding world by observation and reading books to at least get by had passed with the coming of mass society. More was happening that needed to be understood, and yet it became harder and harder to understand.

To supply the need, the mass media were perfected, of which Lippmann's own syndicated political column was a serious and admirable instance. But as newspapers, magazines, radio, advertising, and television more and more provided the citizenry with images of an increasingly complex world that was never experienced directly they acquired the power not just to report the facts but to create them. They began to make what Daniel Boorstin, the historian and librarian, called "pseudo-events," in a famous book of the same name. Pseudo-events are images more true and real than what used to be called reality. "Vivid image came to overshadow pale reality. Sound motion pictures in color led a whole generation of pioneering American movie-goers to think of Benjamin Disraeli as an earlier imitation of George Arliss, just as television has led a later generation of television watchers to see the Western cowboy as an inferior replica of John Wayne. The Grand Canyon itself became a disappointing reproduction of the Kodachrome original." Images supplied by the media are "more interesting and more attractive than spontaneous events," and so for modern Americans, Boorstin continues, "fantasy is more real than reality," and "the image has more dignity than its original."

The pseudo-event favors the image and the sound over the printed word, and "linguistic" authority now has to be understood in terms of TV and VCRs, video disks and cassettes, where the most significant signs in modern culture are seen and heard rather than read. The word may even, we are beginning to learn, always have by itself been a bit semantically emaciated. Albert Mehrabian has, for example, done some interesting studies suggesting that in public situations people only weight *what* is said at 7 percent, while vocal inflection accounts for 38 percent, and facial expression 55 percent of the total understanding.

Only when Samuel Johnson got involved in a controversy with the earl of Chesterfield did the full political and social dimensions of his dictionary, which had hitherto seemed a purely intellectual and commercial venture, begin to open up. And only when linguistic theories of language like deconstruction are looked at in the full linguistic scene of modern culture, of literacy crises, pseudo-events, advertising, and makeovers, of Watergate, Pentagon press releases, and negative campaign TV spots, do we begin to realize that there are political and social issues of great importance involved in what usually seem only academic matters. In this context it becomes possible to get some perspective on these theories by seeing them not in their usual isolation but in contrast to competing views of language, and to judge them, if not for their "truth," then for their usefulness and for their accuracy in describing the actualities of words at work in the world.

Seen from this angle, literature is at its usual game, offering in this instance a theory of language that directly opposes what is believed about and done with language in the immediate world of experience and ordinary life. Deep below the surface, the linguistic deconstructor and the Madison Avenue account executive may share a cynical view of the emptiness and the malleability of words, but on the working surface of the world at the level of practical affairs they could not be more at odds. One says that language has no truth in it, the other says that language makes truth. One says that texts are endlessly ambiguous and interpreted differently by each reader, the other that the message actually conditions the audience to buy this or vote for that. The literary view of language is analytical and deeply pessimistic. Taking reading as the normal linguistic situation, deconstruction reads the word with scrupulous, indeed agonizing, care. Under these intense interpretive pressures, grammar, logic, and rhetoric break down, contradictions appear in every statement, meaning is endlessly deferred, ambivalence is in every word, emptiness appears below every construction, and meaning ultimately collapses. Language examined from this direction appears either a fraud or an illusion, and the world that it names and orders disintegrates into distant and retreating fragments.

Communication in the public world, in television for example, is a much more rough and ready business. Words, carrying only a part of the meaning, are backed up by visual images and surrounded with various kinds of explanatory context. The image makers and verbal engineers are pragmatic and cheerfully optimistic, thinking of language as speech or as some simple form of the printed word like journalism or advertising jingles. Words are in movement and interactive, self-correcting, so that not only is there no time to pause and consider the refinements of grammar and logic, there is no need to be concerned with illogicalities and contradictions, which cut very little ice because any difficulties with them will be either unnoticed or easily straightened out. Above all, the image makers have no doubt that words work, that they convey information with considerable precision from user to audience, and this linguistic confidence is confirmed every day by the success of advertising campaigns, political image-making, public relations blitzes, and media management of the news.

Politics inevitably gets involved in these different attitudes toward language, communication, and knowledge. The public language, confident in general that things work, tends to support the status quo of which it is a working part, and plays to conventional social beliefs. These views lean to the political right, and television advertisements, for example, seem more often plugs for some commonplace, materialistic version of "the American Way of Life," cheery, trouble-free, sexy, and on wheels, than of the product itself.

Deconstruction's negative views—Nietzschean criticism with a hammer—about normal language, far from being mere aesthetics, are the instrument of aggressive, alienated, left-leaning political and social attitudes. The literary view of language is not only contemptuous of the vulgarity, inaccuracy, and linguistic manipulation of public language, it is radical and revolutionary in its use of language as a metaphor behind which to stalk bigger game. De Man tells us that "in these innocent-looking didactic exercises [of analyzing the contradictions inescapable in language] we are in fact playing for very sizable stakes." Those stakes are nothing less than discrediting the beliefs on which the social order is built, "categories that are said to partake of reality, such as the self, man, society, 'the artist, his culture, and the human community.'" Exploration of the insufficiencies of literary language, de Man says, provides a way of exposing much larger and more deeply "rooted ideologies by revealing the mechanics of their workings." Far from merely investigating semantic indeterminacies, or analyzing the language of literary texts, deconstruction uses these critical exercises to reveal the arbitrariness and artificiality of those "rooted ideologies" that are nothing less than the categories on which the public sense of reality and meaning are built, "the concepts of causality, of the subject, of identity, of referential and revealed truth . . . the metaphors of primacy, of genetic history, and most notably, of the autonomous power to will of the self." Structuralism and deconstruction have been one of the primary means by which literature has been politicized, and exposure of the logical deficiencies of language has been the means used to demystify the ideology of industrial, capitalist society.

Using these linguistic theories, contemporary literature continues to claim the linguistic authority for itself that Samuel Johnson's dictionary established for letters and that romanticism and modernism had maintained with various conceptions of language. But, while structuralism and deconstruction remain intellectually interesting, they have failed to provide a basis on which literature can continue to maintain its authority in language. Literary people blindly refuse to accept that the literary conception of language has gone down a blind alley and that they have removed themselves and their subject from any serious role in shaping the world's language. But the battle is long over, and the world has known it and made it official in, fittingly enough, its dictionaries.

The linguistic tide began running away from great writers and professional men of letters long ago. The Philological Society and Sir James Murray when planning and assembling the successor to Johnson as the authoritative English wordbook, *A New English Dictionary on Historical Principles*, printed between 1884 and 1928, accepted as a principle, according to Murray's biographer, K. M. Elisabeth Murray, that "the literary merit or demerit of any particular writer, like the comparative elegance or inelegance of any given word, is a subject upon which the Lexicographer is bound to be almost indifferent." In practice, however, as Jürgen Schäfer has shown in a book-length study, the *OED* continued to favor the language of writers like Shakespeare, especially those whose importance had been established by earlier reference works. Roy Harris, in a famous *TLS* review in 1982 of one of the supplementary volumes, charged that

> literary snobbery continued to pervade the OED, and by 1972 had hardened into official policy as regards new admissions. If you happened to be a famous author, you could take the liberty of inventing a word, or cribbing one from a foreign language, and your boldness was likely to be held to "enrich" the English language (however absurd, unnecessary or trivial the innovation). But if you were just a reporter writing for the local paper, or a civil servant drafting a document, you apparently had no business introducing new words at all, however useful. This is an editorial policy which will admit almost anything into a dictionary, provided it comes from the prestigious pen of some literary lion— a Samuel Beckett (*athambia*) or a Virginia Woolf (*scrolloping*). No protest against including fun-words in a dictionary is here intended. The point is that the OED's "fun" has to be sanctioned by literary respectability. And the obligatory route to literary respectability is via the printed word.

Even with the appearance in 1989 of the second edition of the world's greatest dictionary in twenty volumes, priced at £1,500, incorporating the four supplemental volumes (but not updating the older entries) prepared over the years, and including slang and obscenities thought too racy for the earlier version, the old "black and white lexicography" remained the rule. The *TLS* reviewer of the second edition in 1989, the poet Geoffrey Hill, caught the tone of the edition exactly when he used the unusually expansive three pages the *TLS* gave him to test nothing but how well the new edition recorded the verbal subtleties of Gerard Manley Hopkins, one of the most linguistically idiosyncratic and subtle poets ever to write in English.

Oxford is still, as Matthew Arnold long ago remarked in *Culture and Anarchy*, in love with lost causes, for while the author may still reign de jure in the *OED*, the de facto transfer of linguistic power that has taken place in the twentieth century had already been acknowledged and recorded in an American dictionary, the third edition of Webster's *New International Dictionary*, published in 1961. Webster's Second, published in 1934, had been a conventional dictionary in its Adamic assumption that there was such a thing as correct English and that the standard English authors and the classics of English literature were the places where it was to be found. Slang and colloquialisms were allowed among the approximately 600,000 entries, but they were firmly marked as second-class words. For the most part only words used by great canonical writers like Shakespeare, Wordsworth, Pope, Shelley, Macaulay, and Milton were considered first-rate, legitimate English words.

Webster's Third was put together on very different principles. The chief editor, Dr. Philip Gove, had earlier been in charge of a Works Progress Administration project that made a card catalog of all the quotations in Johnson's *Dictionary*, presently in the Sterling Library at Yale. But in putting together his own dictionary, Gove accepted the view that a dictionary "must be descriptive and not prescriptive." According to Gove in his preface to Webster's Third, "artificial notions of correctness or superiority" had to be abandoned in a dictionary based on descriptive principles, which meant that in our democratic century, language is what people everywhere and in every walk of life say and mean. The result is a different language from Johnson's or Murray's. The lexicon of Webster's Third is smaller by about 150,000 words than Webster's Second, it contains a great deal more jargon, the lines between slang and polite usage almost disappear, pronunciations and meanings multiply, Latinate terms diminish, etymologies are discounted and many of the sharper semantic distinctions of earlier dictionaries blur considerably.

This latter feature, which attracted the most unfavorable comment at the time of publication, made clear that deifying *sermo cotidianus* involved a considerable blunting of distinctions in the language. Dwight Macdonald, who played the role of Chesterfield to Webster's Third, drew attention in his acid review, "The String Untuned," to the way in which the traditionally distinct meanings of *nauseous/nauseated*, *deprecate/depreciate*, *forcible/forceful*, *unexceptional/unexceptionable*, *disinterested/uninterested* disappeared into one another in Webster's Third. The result of all this, as many at the time saw and lamented, was a more democratic but a less precise, an easier but a less definite language, and one in which there were no standards except the momentary ones of what people said and intended.

Webster's lexicographers defended their work doggedly, and their product remains in force today, the standard dictionary of American English, the language of the most powerful nation and the lingua franca of the world. It is also an accurate representation of linguistic reality in our time, which has small place for the verbal authority of the great writers or their works. Many of them inevitably survived in the pages of Webster's Third, since all dictionaries are made out of other dictionaries, but their views about the meaning of words have no more force there than those of theater people like Billy Rose and Ethel Merman, or professional athletes like Ted Williams, or advertising account executives, lawyers, broadcasters, politicians, and on and on. Nor did printed books have any linguistic priority over briefer forms like newspaper articles and journals, or over the spoken word as it was heard on radio and television, and reported in interviews. Even as Johnson's dictionary recorded and furthered the transfer of linguistic authority from the aristocracy to the profession of writing, so Webster's Third marked and hastened the transfer in our time of linguistic authority from printed literature to the public media and those who control them.

Webster's Third made it official, in a relatively pale and bloodless way, but the literary world continues to fight a bitter rearguard action for the control of language. An entire industry, of which the George Orwell of Newspeak is the patron saint, and "Politics and the English Language" the sacred text, has grown up to try to contain what is treated as a verbal meltdown. Edwin Newman, William Safire (sometime speech writer for Spiro Agnew!), John Simon, and others write regular columns prophesying the end of civilization because infinitives are split and can/may and should/would are no longer distinguished. The National Council of the Teachers of English has formed a doublespeak taskforce to combat the onset of linguistic barbarism, Richard Mitchell of Glassboro State College publishes a pamphlet titled the *Underground Grammarian*, and the *Chronicle of Higher Education* prints satiric exposés by crazed English teachers with such titles as "I Can't Teech Comp No More." But the real resistance, fierce and undeterred by its lack of effect or by the defection of the lexicographers to the language engineers and the financial and political interests they serve, remains literature and its present-day institutional conception of public language as an empty pretense. The moment of truth for these literary-intellectual views came in a recent event that not only was conclusive in what it showed about the relation of language to the world outside the text but also demonstrated the real gut issues that are at stake in theories of language.

Paul de Man, who died in 1983, was very much a mandarin, a retiring but charismatic teacher of literature to the elite at Harvard,

Cornell, Johns Hopkins, and Yale. In the later years of his career he was one of the leaders in the deconstructive criticism, to which he brought a philologist's exquisite ability to tease opposing significations from texts. Born in Belgium in 1919, he emigrated to the United States a few years after the Second World War ended and, after working for a time in New York and teaching at a nearby college, made his way through Harvard Graduate School, studying comparative literature and becoming a member of the prestigious Society of Fellows. One distinguished appointment followed another, and at Yale in the 1970s and 1980s, where his work in deconstruction flowered, he became a scholar of world renown and a teacher of extraordinary power, able by the force of his intellect and his charming personality to form extraordinarily strong bonds with his graduate students. His powers in all respects were quite out of the ordinary and had to be experienced directly for their full force to be appreciated. His death from cancer at age sixty-four was widely felt as a tragedy.

De Man's theories would have remained in the ivory tower had it not been for a scandal that broke soon after his death. In 1987, a Belgian student looking for dissertation material turned up a number of journalistic pieces on cultural matters written by de Man in the early 1940s, during the German occupation of Belgium, for newspapers controlled by the Germans and employed for fascist propaganda. These pieces were by no means the crudest kind of propaganda, but they did follow the Nazi party line, from a left- rather than a right-wing orientation, on crucial matters like racial characteristics, the necessity of putting the good of the state over the interests of the individual, the German role in civilizing Europe, and the necessity of accepting and working with the new world order. In all these many pieces, there was one particularly terrible essay, "Les Juifs dans la Littérature actuelle," published in the German-controlled paper *Le Soir* on March 4, 1941, in which de Man argued that since the Jews had contributed nothing to European literature, "on voit donc qu'une solution du problème juif qui viserait à la création d'une colonie juive isolée de l'Europe, n'entraînerait pas, pour la vie littéraire de l'Occident, de conséquences déplorables" (it follows that a solution to the Jewish question which envisages the creation of a Jewish colony isolated from Europe would not lead to deplorable consequences for the literary life of the West). Were the Jews to be sent to Madagascar, or one of the other places "isolated from Europe" then being discussed, de Man concludes, Western culture "would lose, all told, a few [literary] personalities of mediocre value and would continue, as in the past, to develop according to its own great evolutionary principles." The "solution to the Jewish problem" was not, of course, to be some "colonie juive isolée de l'Europe" but concentration camps like Auschwitz and Dachau and their gas chambers. One of these camps used for gathering Jews for shipment to the East was already in place in Belgium when de Man wrote, though there is no certainty that he knew of it.

As knowledge of the early writings of de Man spread, the scandal grew and more circumstances came to light. Paul de Man's uncle, Henri de Man, to whom he was very close, had been a Quisling of high rank, though a very odd one. It was most unusual for someone of de Man's age and experience to be allowed to write for the most important political journals of the time. He escaped being sent in one of the "voluntary" labor contingents from Belgium to the German factories that were the fate of many of his age. Further poking about resulted in a long article by James Atlas in the *New York Times Magazine* (August 28, 1988) reporting that de Man had at the end of the war gone to New York after being involved in some murky business dealings in a publishing venture in Belgium. He separated from his wife and three children—at least they went to South America when he came to New York—and the family was not reunited. After gaining a teaching position at Bard College with the help of various New York literati, notably Mary McCarthy, he remarried, probably before there was a divorce. For many years all this scandalous past had been buried, apparently not known to even his intimates. Even now these events are blurred and uncertain, largely because of the determined unwillingness of de Man's many friends and admirers to go into them, or to allow others to do so. There was an effort to denounce him as a collaborator when he applied for a passport after entering graduate training at Harvard, but in a letter that apparently satisfied the professor, Renato Poggioli, in charge of the Society of Fellows, de Man countered the charges of his unidentified accuser.

And with this the past disappeared, altogether, until de Man's later fame caused a graduate student combing the archives in Belgium to notice and call attention to the fatal articles by his famous countryman. (Graduate students wandering in the stacks in search of dissertation topics are becoming one of the major hazards in academic life.) Once known, the issue brought into play the strongest feelings of all interested parties. Paul de Man's many good friends, the former students who felt extraordinarily close to him, and the many literary people with a professional and political commitment to deconstruction denied that what de Man had written during the war was a very serious matter, or even if it was, that there was no real connection between the young man's folly and his later, serious work. The earlier pieces were written, it was argued, when he was very young, in a time of great confusion and fear. They were not nearly so bad as what other people were writing anyway. Let the dead bury the dead. Above all, de Man's apologists insisted that there was no connection between de Man's early political views, even if he had been a collaborator, and his later literary theories, despite their indebtedness to writers with connections to Nazi theories like Nietzsche and Heidegger. Ideas and life are distinct from one another, they contended, as literary people always do. Might as well attack Rousseau's views, on which de Man had written eloquently, about the innate goodness of man by bringing up the fact that he forced his mistress to send all their children to a home for foundlings!

"Les Juifs dans la Littérature actuelle" was itself deconstructed by the father of deconstruction and de Man's close friend, the French philosopher-critic Jacques Derrida, to demonstrate that its linguistic contradictions and semantic insufficiencies allowed it to be interpreted as not support for but a demystification of Nazi political positions. Defenders like Derrida were particularly concerned to show that de Man's deconstructive theories about the absence of a definitive meaning in words and texts cannot be taken as a defense erected in later life against the guilt of what had been written in youth. If words can't mean any definite thing, then de Man's earlier writings never *really* meant any single thing, like solving the "Jewish problem," and therefore no harm was done. De Man's defenders are not really much happier with a softer psychological explanation that has been offered portraying his deconstructive theories as de Man's mature rejection of a youthful commitment to a murderous absolute ideology by discrediting all such "totalizing" or "essentializing" theories.

On the other hand, those hostile to de Man and to deconstruction insisted that de Man had written something definitely anti-Semitic in a time when the Jews of Europe were being slaughtered, and that there simply is no way of ignoring or explaining away what they view as knowing collaboration and opportunism. This argument usually goes on to insist that his later literary theories cannot be separated from his earlier life but have to be seen as an elaborate strategy carefully developed over a lifetime to deny to himself and others that he had done anything, or even that anything had happened. As Stanley Corngold put it feelingly, "de Man's critical work [deconstruction] makes good sense, once it has been identified as his carapace and portable house. But to continue to teach it while pretending to forget its beginnings in Nazi collaboration is to play out a masquerade—a life that is, then, precisely only a text."

Considering de Man's own demystifications of the concepts of the self and "the knowing, willing subject," it is ironic how real his personality was and is, even after death. It lives on in the vehement determination of his friends to justify *him* and his enemies to damn *him* as a man. Most discussions of the matter get right down to what *he* was and did. But we can never know his motives, and it would seem we have no choice but to let him go and settle for the facts, which are quite remarkable enough. What cannot be blinked in *l'affaire de Man* is the power of words to endure and even to "speak with most miraculous organ." Brief pieces of trivial daily journalism in the first place, reading consumables written to earn a living and entertain the mass audience, propaganda designed to serve the political moment, they lay there in the dusty stacks of the library for fifty years, until like Nemesis, or "pat . . . like the catastrophe of the old comedy," as Edmund puts it in *Lear*, with all the incredible precision of Cocteau's infernal machine, their moment came. And when it did, language spoke like the voice of the oracle in ancient tragedy, not with the simple meanings of the original words, but with all the almost unbearable ironic force that the Holocaust and the events of the past fifty years have now given to "on voit donc qu'une solution du problème juif qui viserait à la création d'une colonie juive isolée de l'Europe, n'entraînerait pas, pour la vie littéraire de l'Occident, de conséquences déplorables."

So powerful are these words that they have generated a flood of other words in magazines and newspapers, at learned conferences and in scholarly journals, reprints of all the journalism de Man had written as a young man, collections of his later critical writings, no matter how minute, and article after article poring over every possible detail, offering every possible interpretation of what had happened and what it meant. Perhaps because deconstruction has always had a flavor of the satanic, and because old Nazis like Klaus Barbie and Kurt Waldheim were turning up at the time of the de Man scandal in a final settling of old accounts, the media picked up the de Man story and published more words about it. Books being published about this time about the German philosopher Heidegger, questioning the connection between his phenomenological philosophy and his Nazi politics, directed even more attention toward de Man and the question of whether there was some link between fascism and deconstruction, which had roots in continental phenomenology. Scholars closely associated with deconstruction and friends to de Man were particularly sensitive to this issue, and there were heated exchanges about it in the journals and discussions at various conferences. Eventually all, or all the found, pieces of de Man's wartime journalism, something over 183, were published in a huge volume, *Paul de Man's Wartime Journalism, 1939–1943*. And then in 1989, a companion volume, *Responses on Paul de Man's Wartime Journalism* appeared (478 double-column folio pages, with a detailed chronology of events in wartime Belgium) with 38 essays pro and con exploring with extraordinary thoroughness all the many aspects of the question.

In this rapidly expanding verbal setting, de Man's earlier deconstructive theories discounting any reality outside the text—the "debilitating burden of paraphrase," the "literary dimensions of language [are] largely obscured if one submits uncritically to the authority of reference," the "myth of semantic correspondence between sign and referent," a "preventative semiological hygiene"—took on the tragic tone of Sophoclean hubris. Some deconstructive indeterminacy might hang about de Man's motives, but the "correspondence between sign and referent," far from being a myth, became an overwhelming reality. His rediscovered words brought back into being, as if they had always been there waiting, never really having disappeared into what we call the past, a flood of the smallest details of the world in which his journalism was written. Defending and attacking him, the scholars described the Belgian concentration camp and the shipments of Jews to it, the numbers in the labor battalions going to Germany and the dates of their departure, the German takeover of the Belgian media, the editorial policy and the writers for *Le Soir*, its nickname, *Le Soir*

Volé, the politics of de Man's uncle and his place in the government, exactly where de Man lived, how he got his apartment, his relationships with other members of the family, his effort to escape from Europe in 1940, and on and on. Far from there being nothing outside of the text, everything was out there, waiting to be called back into reality by the power of words. Of all the events evoked by de Man's words, the Holocaust was most intensely real, of course, and the determination of the Jews that it would not be forgotten, or diminish in memory to some trivial event, ensured that de Man's words about the *problème juif* would not and could not escape what he mocked as the "authority of reference," ensured that his words, whatever their logical status, would forever be tied to and derive their meaning from events in the world.

The de Man case removes deconstruction from the realm of pure intellect and puts the theory, protesting and wriggling, in a full living human context. It confronts deconstruction with the monstrous and passionately felt *fact* of the Holocaust and asks, is this too only a *text*? Can its meaning be endlessly deferred? Can it too be interpreted in any way deemed suitable? To all these questions, of course, despite the staggering revelations of the de Man case, the logician can and does answer "yes." The deconstructors continue to prove that words are indeterminate, that any text has a surplus of meaning, that interpretations are infinite and arbitrary, and that the world perceived by consciousness is nothing more than a series of ephemeral texts. Examined from this perspective, language is always breaking down, crumbling into nothingness, revealing traces, holes, contradictions, conventionality, infinite regress, tautology, nothing outside the text, ahistoricity, the metaphysics of presence where there is only absence, indeterminacy, logocentrism, différence, the need for supplemention, and numerous other logical weaknesses.

The language of the world where things are done and made and sold looks at language from a practical rather than a strictly logical viewpoint. The result is an awe-inspiring, often daunting, linguistic overconfidence, sometimes cynical and exploitative, regularly immoral, irreverent, and greedy, but quick, clever, thoroughly alert to the possibilities of what can be done with words. Words are not pale isolated things but magical in their ability to evoke, shape, control things. To the eye of the philosopher it is all a vast swindle, but what privileges the casuistries of the philosopher over the evidence of all our lives to decide what is real and true? Words work in the world, they make people rich and poor, happy and sad, wise and foolish, and what better proof can there be of their meaningfulness and power?

There have been past times when literature has been the leading voice in this kind of linguistic activism, populated with those who have like Shakespeare's characters "eat paper and drunk ink," or like Jonson's scoundrels maximized the nomenclatures, or like Dickens's people spoke in all the accents of the world, or like Joyce juggled *all* the words. But those days are seemingly gone, and literature, both in practice and theory, has cast its lot with a negative view of language, offering itself no longer as Shakespeare's "great feast of languages" but as the empty gabble of Beckett's stage or the pale fire of the Nabokovian novel. Of course we no longer live in the dawn of pure linguistic enthusiasm, we have heard too many words, and learned to distrust them. But though it would not appear so from our poetry and novels, the world is still filled with confidence in words. Which side is likely to prevail, which view comes closest to the situation in which we actually live and with which literature should be identified, became overwhelmingly clear in the tragedy of Paul de Man's writings.

8

The Tree of Knowledge:

Literature's Presence

in the Social World

Language commits us willy-nilly to statements like "literature *is* this," or "*literature* is that," that objectify and essentialize literature. Both the general public and those committed professionally to writing and to literary study regularly speak and write as if literature were a definite objective thing that can be located, analyzed, and described in a scientific manner. Even our modern skeptics, the deconstructionists, offer theories of literature that tacitly take it for, or at least speak of it as, some definite objective reality. "The literary text simultaneously asserts and denies the authority of its own rhetorical mode." Since literature has no objective reality and there is no hard social agreement about what it is, a great many discussions past and present about what literature is have been as pointless as they have been indecisive.

Literature is real enough, but it exists only fragmentarily, primarily in a canon of texts accepted at a given time as literary, but also in such pieces as the biographies of authors, critical discussions and literary histories, a university course of study, aesthetics, reviews, literary journals, legalities such as copyright and the rights of artists, conceptions of language, the "P" category in the Library of Congress classification system, and on and on. Theories about it have been as various as its components. It has been said to be the expression of certain psychological faculties—creative imagination or id—or the elaboration of particular formal properties—metaphor or metonymy—or a specific relation of words to reality—fictive, mimetic, or symbolic.

Literature was firmed up considerably and defined more sharply in the nineteenth and twentieth centuries by being institutionalized in the university curriculum, in various romantic and modern poetic theories, and in a library classification category. But its parts, various, incoherent, and changeable, remain an eclectic combination of texts of infinite variety, primitive epics, religious tracts, state propaganda, love songs, dirges, and on and on. Subjectively, no two people agree precisely or altogether on what it is. No individual thinks of it without mistiness and contradictions. No group ever quite establishes a total literary program. Objectively, its forms are never stable or complete. There are recurrent symmetries like poetry and prose, or persistent genre patterns like lyric, epic, dramatic, but the definitions and formal properties of these literary types vary, and the pieces are never assembled in a coherent and complete system. As with all cultural things, there is never time or energy or interest or agreement enough to put literature *all* together, and so it remains eternally incomplete. Located in no single place, it is more activity than thing. Constantly working and changing, it is not some Platonic idea of literature or Hegelian literary *Geist* revealing itself in the process of time, but more a Wittgensteinian series in which the first and last members share no formal characteristics but are connected only by being parts of a history of change. It retains portions of the past, but always adapts them to new circumstances, needs, and interests. Once poetry and rhetoric, then belles lettres and polite letters, now literature, perhaps soon to be something else as yet unnamed.

To understand literature's unavoidable lack of objectivity is to begin to see the futility of discussions of literature that assume, as almost all writing about literature does, either explicitly or implicitly, that there is some *thing* we call literature and that it can be described accurately or inaccurately. I am not objecting to the kind of loose linguistic generalizing that makes discussion possible—"literature's unavoidable lack of objectivity"—a type of statement I have used many times in these pages. I am only saying that no one should confuse this kind of rhetorical nominalization with literal truth and waste time arguing about what literature *is* or *is not*. What we can do, with some degree of surety that we are engaged in a meaningful activity, is to accept that all literary activity, the writing of a poem, the construction of a systematic poetics, the teaching of a literary work, the assembling of a piece of literary history such as the present book, is finally only an argument that it would be plausible, appropriate, and useful to think of literature, for the moment at least, as this or that. Literary description is not and cannot be a science—there is no object firm and coherent enough to be analyzed—but it can be a way of giving literature a particular spin and making it real in the social world in a particular way.

Where else, finally, can literature exist but as a social reality? An innate idea? A Platonic form? An a priori category like Kantian beauty or Freudian id-ego exchange? A mental faculty like the creative imagination? Or even, more modestly, an unchanging group of canonical texts with identical literary properties? All these transcendental possibilities have by now been tried and exhausted, and the future of literature, if there is to be one, would seem to depend on first grasping clearly and firmly, and then working on the basis of the fact that literature is a floating and changing social reality, existing partly in consciousness and partly in fragmentary objectivations organized in a rudimentary institutional form. There are, of course, a number of social theories of culture, more often than not nowadays some variety of Marxism, but they usually limit the culture-society relationship to some mechanical interaction and reduce the motivation for the construction of social reality to a conspiracy driven by little more than greed or a will to power. But a social theory of culture in general, and literature and the arts in particular, if it is to have any use, must comprehend the complexity of the socially constructed reality or *Lebenswelt* while offering literature and the arts a place of dignity in that reality. And it must also give credit to the positive human need to give meaning to individual and collective life. An adequate social theory must also take into account the intricacy and clever opportunism with which human beings put social life together. Earlier chapters have offered several small-scale empirical studies of various complex ways in which literature and the other arts are woven into the cultural web, and I want now to offer a concluding example of one large-scale and important way in which literature has been built into the social order. The example of the "knowledge tree" not only suggests how complex and indirect are the ways of making literature socially real but also makes clear how critical it is for literature to be fully conscious of and respond in a positive way to its inescapable social status.

Literature belongs not to nature but to the world of culture that Vico, who, along with Hobbes, is sometimes honored as our first sociologist, believed we can understand fully because it was made by humans for human purposes. We cannot completely comprehend light or matter, he tells us, since they are parts of nature originating outside the human; but we can understand mathematics or language or literature since they are made by human beings for human purposes. Human products are understandable, for example, as teleological, designed to go somewhere for some purpose, which can be as simple as completing a chronological sequence, or as complex as the gradual revelation of a divine order.

In the nineteenth century, Wilhelm Dilthey formalized Vico's theory by dividing knowledge between *Geisteswissenschaften*, composed of various subjects like history, anthropology, economics, and literature that have as their object of study the ideographic, or the "objectivations of the mind," and *Naturwissenschaften*, or the hard sciences that have as their object the nomothetic, or the study of nature. Dilthey's realm of geist is the socially constructed, meaningful reality hypothesized by what is now known as the sociology of knowledge, a Lebenswelt made up of humanly constructed institutions, objects, and consciousness, ranging from architecture to ethical systems and arts like literature. In this realm, in H. P. Rickman's words,

> the human mind can understand whatever it has created and the whole historical world spreads before us as a field of human activity, of the realization of human hopes and the suffering of misery and frustration by human beings. The natural scientist observes sequences of events and construes causal or other laws from them. In history we not only know that somebody saw the chance of a crown and acted to gain it, but also what it is to want something, to strive for it, which forms the inner link between these events. Not only the facts but also the connections between them lie open before us.

In this social scene where people make war and worship gods, build cities, write poems, paint pictures, and stage plays in order to give their lives meaning, people always try, of course, to make their constructs seem given and factual, not artificial, to the eye of the beholder. Religion, for example, creates and integrates theologies, churches, rituals, sacred books, sacraments, vestments, church history, catechisms, priestly hierarchies, sacred art, religious education, excommunication, canon law, and all the many ideas, things, and activities that constitute its reality, to make itself seem not an artifice but a fact of being, given by God and developing historically in the world. Not only religion but all culture regularly presents itself as in sociobiology, or *natural* law, as if discovered by science, not invented by human art. Even when the artificiality of culture is at least half-acknowledged, it is still thought better to have at least one foot in nature, in sexual practices, for example, though perhaps less so in table manners. And the naturalization of culture works, for in the consciousness of those who are born and live within it, who believe its truths and die for its political values, culture is totally real. Its language names and organizes an actual world, its kinship structures are facts of blood, its calendar is time, its metaphysics are reality, its cities and gardens are the landscape, and its art is truth and beauty.

The concept of the socially constructed reality of the Lebenswelt exposes culture's masquerade as nature, but it leaves such cultural realities as literature and the other arts an honorable place in the social scheme of things as a useful partner in making a meaningful world in which to live in the face of a nature going relentlessly and invariably on its meaningless way. In the human scene conceived in this way, individual literary works organize life in a purposeful fashion, as Dickens made sense of the difficult business of living in a huge and impersonal nineteenth-century city. Such individual literary works as Dickens's novels are a part of the total institution of literature—the literary texts plus the lives of the poets, the teaching of literature, and all the many other components of literary reality—which organizes an important field of human activity, that of writing, or even more broadly, of using words, and directs it toward the general social aim of constructing some kind of believable and acceptable Lebenswelt.

Literature, in turn, acquires social reality, becomes present in the world, by virtue of its participation in this project, interacting, in ways we have sampled in earlier chapters, with politics, law, technology, language, education, literacy, property, plagiarism, individual creativity, and other cultural institutions and ways of thinking about important things. Its existence is intertwined with these other social realities, and its fortunes are tied to them. When they shift, literature moves, and were they to cease to recognize literature's existence the result would be ontologically catastrophic. Were the category "literature" to be removed from the Library of Congress classification system, to use an apocalyptic example, literature would crash into an abyss of nonbeing far darker than that contemplated, with an intellectual frisson, by deconstruction. Such a cultural catastrophe is unthinkable, at least for the moment, but lesser disasters are not inconceivable. It is entirely possible, for example, that literature might in the near future lose its place in the official system of knowledge, the knowledge tree, that has been particularly important to its social reality in the modern world, giving it firm status as a body of truth and a way of knowing truth.

Meaning, not raw facts, is what humanity seeks, and society is a collection of kits or codes for processing raw facts into meaning. Ordering is one of the simplest and most durable human methods for finding or making meaning. Take a variety of things and put them in some kind of relationship, a simple sequence, a taxonomy, a hierarchy, or a cause-and-effect pattern, say, and they make sense, apparently for no better reason than the tautological one that order and relationship are felt by human beings to be meaningful. Psychological explanations of an "ordering instinct" can be and have been offered, but they are not necessary. It is an overwhelmingly obvious fact that human societies order things in simple and elaborate ways. The periodic table of elements, the Indo-European family of languages, the ten commandments, the multiplication table, the metric system, the Linnean taxonomy of plants: so extensive are its charts, tables, structures, and classification systems that culture can be said to be composed of an extensive series of interlocking schemes of order.

The ultimate aim of society might well be viewed, not as the scientific explanation of an a priori reality, though this is the orthodox definition of knowledge in our scientific age, but as assembling all these individual systems into a master system of knowledge, a unified field not of physical forces but of culture. It seems beyond us at the moment, and perhaps happily so, but we can glimpse such a total

how we codify & who we are in process of codification

system of meaning distantly, for example, in the ruins of Mayan civilization, where all human affairs, including massive architecture, a language of religious symbols, a numbering system, agriculture, and elaborate rituals, were correlated with a complex calendar, and ultimately with the stars. Western civilization may have come closest to a total order in the so-called Great Chain of Being described by its historian, A. O. Lovejoy, as,

> the conception of the plan and structure of the world which, through the Middle Ages and down to the late eighteenth century, many philosophers, most men of science, and, indeed, most educated men, were to accept without question. The . . . "Great Chain of Being" [was] composed of an immense, or—by the strict but seldom rigorously applied logic of the principle of continuity—of an infinite number of links ranging in hierarchical order from the meagerest kind of existents, which barely escape nonexistence, through every possible grade up to the *ens perfectissimum.*

Broken links of the Great Chain are still lying about modern culture—the lion as king of the beasts, the influences of astrological figures, the jewels appropriate to certain anniversaries, the four basic elements—earth, air, fire, and water—and the temperaments or humors, choleric, sanguine, bilious, and melancholic. Since the Renaissance, however, the old mechanical metaphors of chains and ladders have been replaced by more organic imagery, particularly the "tree," suggesting that systems of classification are natural, not artificial, and that as such they have the potential to grow and develop. Perhaps, too, the metaphor carries a hint of the Faustian danger of knowledge as

> the Fruit
> Of that Forbidden Tree, whose mortal taste
> Brought Death into the World, and all our woe.

Trees, such as the familiar scheme diagraming the Darwinian evolution of species, have been for a long time the principal organizational images for all kinds of information. No tree has been more important than the knowledge tree, which limits and organizes what are considered at any given time to be the legitimate categories and methods of true understanding. There were many knowledge trees, but the one that has been most influential in shaping the modern conception of knowledge appeared in 1751 in the introductory section of the first volume of the *Encyclopédie*. Diderot and d'Alembert divided knowledge into three categories, each based on a distinct mental faculty: memory, reason, and imagination. These psychological categories branched out into particular types of discourse, memory into history, reason into philosophy, and imagination into poetry. In turn, these discursive genres exfoliated into various subgroups, and they in turn into others, and so on. Poetry, used in Diderot's tree in the broad sense still current as the term for all creative work without regard for the medium—what we more often nowadays call "art"—branched out into the various fine arts, which were at that time being defined in something like the modern manner as literature, music, painting, sculpture, theater, and engraving. Over time, of course, additional arts have been added, architecture and dance in earlier times and more recently, photography and film.

Trees—"decision trees," for example—are still familiar, but not so intellectually fashionable or convincing as they once were, and the most authoritative schematizations of knowledge nowadays appear in practical forms such as the classification systems of large libraries, particularly national systems such as that of the Library of Congress or the British Library. The principal modern knowledge tree is, however, the academic structure of major universities as recorded in the catalog with its listing of divisions, departments, and curricula. The university not only in general objectifies human intelligence—a matter that always needs reinforcement—but, in the divisions and departments of study, certifies certain modes of knowledge as genuine—astronomy, not astrology—and orders them in relation to one another.

In the modern university cum knowledge tree, there have been persistent tangles, like the point where biology, chemistry, and physics meet, or where minority and political groups seek recognition as subjects. But the basic paradigm has remained relatively unchanged for about the past hundred years since the establishment of the modern multiversity on the German model. There are regularly three, sometimes four, divisions of arts and sciences: natural sciences, sometimes further divided into the physical and biological sciences, the social sciences, and the humanities. In the academic hierarchy the natural sciences take precedence, reflecting their almost absolute authority as a mode of knowledge. The social subjects that like to think of themselves as most empirical, such as psychology and economics, in times of greatest confidence in themselves have sought, without success, transfer to the division of physical sciences. There are very real rewards for being a science of any kind, and history, once a humanity almost everywhere, now perceives advantage in being a social science. Humanities—music, philosophy, classics, literature, the "old" subjects—because of their collective failure, discussed in chapter 2, to systematize their objects and methods of study in a scientific manner, continue to be taken as the softest modes of knowledge in the university world.

These divisions, natural sciences, social sciences, and humanities, each in turn divided up into several departments, constitute the Arts and Sciences, traditionally the most prestigious because the most abstract or "pure" forms of knowledge. In the full-scale university, as opposed to the college, they are surrounded by the various professional schools, such as engineering, law, and medicine, which are said to concern themselves less with theory than with practical skills and applied forms of knowledge.

The university is not just an instructional institution but a living knowledge tree, a practical and active way not only of recording the official order of knowledge but for reviewing new claims to epistemological authority and adjusting the knowledge paradigm to developing concepts. As Robert Darnton (1985) says, "Pigeon-holing is an exercise in power," and nowhere more so than in the controlled, but nonetheless bitter, fights within universities over what kinds of study can go into the departmental pigeonhole and thereby be validated as true types of knowledge. The angry struggles of recent years for departmental status by women's studies, black studies, Jewish studies, and other specialized subjects—peace or environment—testify to how critical the matter is conceived to be. There are, of course, immediate practical advantages. Departments are a matter of status and patronage, money and jobs, budgetary and appointment powers. But beyond these realities, to achieve departmental status is to be recognized as an official mode of knowledge. For a subject to become a department is to be legitimated as a fully accepted category of reality, to be declared officially one of the ways of knowing things that are true and a part of what it is important to know. Only full departmental status confers a place in the knowledge tree, and to be made a center or a program, which has usually been the fate of women's and black studies, in contrast, say, to computer science, which made it into the inner circle without impediment, is to be marked as occupying a subsidiary place in the scheme of knowledge and of reality as defined by the university curriculum. Everyone fully understands, though it is seldom said, that the staunch refusal of many major university faculties, under considerable political pressure as those whom society has empowered to make such judgments, to give departmental status to either women's studies or black studies constitutes a judgment that these subjects are more ideology than knowledge. The battle rages furiously, and is likely to get much fiercer as increasingly politicized faculties seek to further their ideological and economic aims by getting departmental status for various social causes, but for the moment the university knowledge tree distinguishes between knowing something and getting something. Those who are clamoring to get departmental status insist, of course, that knowing is only an established way of getting, and there is, of course, no reason why in future the knowledge tree may not bud and branch in many directions, as it has often in the past.

To have no official place whatsoever in the university table of organization, or to lose a place once had, is obviously catastrophic for any subject, a decertification as knowledge, a sentence to nonexistence of the kind that geography has suffered in recent times, or that chemistry worries about, probably needlessly, as physics continues to offer more fundamental explanations of the organization of matter. The difficulty and the importance of getting literature into the standard university curriculum in the late nineteenth century, described in chapter 2, can be better appreciated when we realize that inclusion in the official knowledge tree was at stake in Oxford in 1887. Once literature was a part of the curriculum it was taken much more seriously than it had been heretofore, and it was certified as a true and important way of knowing. Its components—poems, plays, novels—were officially recognized to have something meaningful to say about human affairs, and, even more crucially, the ways of thinking and writing that were considered literary were declared to be serious and fruitful ways of analyzing and recording certain aspects of reality. Literature, in short, became knowledge, and in doing so found a place of some importance in the world.

It remains to be seen whether literature can maintain its place in society's knowledge tree, which is to say in the academic table of organization. Its presence in the university curriculum is highly unstable at the moment. Not only does it continue to fail to meet the academic requirement that true knowledge define the object it studies and systematize its analytic method to at least some modest degree, but it seems to have chosen a disruptive role within the system. Deconstructive philosophical terrorist, intellectual revolutionary, and feminist freedom-fighter are probably only the fashions of the moment, but the insistence that literature has no meaning, or has any meaning the reader cares to give it, wears away the positive authority and even the reality of the subject, as do the charges of the Marxists and feminists that it has been no more than the ideological instrument of various coercive powers seeking to repress freedom and fairness in the interests of power.

These postures make university faculties and administrations understandably nervous about what kind of knowledge is to be found in literature and what the value is in teaching it. Programmatic skepticism probably has no long-term future in educational institutions based on the idea of discovering and teaching positive knowledge. But beneath this surface froth there are deeper and stronger currents running away from the conception of literature as a particular kind of imaginative writing embodying a particular kind of knowledge that has enabled it to occupy a place in the official knowledge tree of modern society. The continuing shift in almost all colleges and universities away from the teaching of literature to the teaching of writing of various kinds signals a de facto change that manifests its direction clearly only in the very large number of universities where there are departments of communication but no departments of English or French literature. It is significant that communications departments appear in the newer and less prestigious educational institutions, for they are the ones most likely to be free enough of tradition to be able to do what seems to make sense, and they are the ones who have to satisfy the real and immediate market demands of their students. To those students and in their institutions, literature is disappearing into another category of reality where it is becoming only one technique for written communication, one among many ways, oral, pictorial, schematic, and many modes, print, television, radio, VCR, cassette, record, and CD, by which information can be assembled, organized, and transmitted effectively.

A generation ago any self-respecting university, no matter how new, would, even as it had a physics or psychology department, have had a large literary component in its curriculum. That this decidedly is no longer the case suggests very pressingly that literature is in the process of losing a place in the knowledge tree and therefore in danger of breaking up in the social world. In its place, apparently, people are beginning to see "communications," a subject with both practical and theoretical dimensions, and considerable usefulness.

Epilogue

In an earlier book, *The Imaginary Library,* I collected for consideration a few of the stories that some of our most important modern writers told in the 1950s and 1960s to express the sense that what they had known as literature was ceasing to be meaningful any longer, disappearing even from the social world and from consciousness. These writers shared a crisis of confidence in some of the most fundamental values that had undergirded literature since the late eighteenth and early nineteenth centuries, such as the belief in writing and creating art as near sacred callings, the visionary power of the imagination, the perfect form and the truth of the literary text, the total communication of writer and reader through literary language, the inalienable presence of a mystically true meaning at the center of the literary work of art, and, finally, the epistemological superiority of imaginative literature to science or any other factual form of discourse. A story Norman Podhoretz tells about Robert Lowell illustrates the kind of beliefs involved and the certainty with which they were held to the end by many literary people.

> He [Lowell] was always getting involved in political battles, but in my opinion the only thing that was real to him was poetry, and it was only through poetry that anything else ever became real. He once said to me in answer to certain criticisms I had made of the poetry of W. H. Auden in the course of a quiet conversation:

"After all, if not for Auden we wouldn't have known about the Second World War." At first I was puzzled by the remark, and then it struck me that he meant it literally: if *he* had never read about the outbreak of the war in Auden's poem "September 1, 1939," if he had only read about it in a newspaper, he would never have believed in its reality.

But Lowell, himself a *monstre sacré* of art, was among the last to believe such things about literature, and a number of his contemporaries were already portraying the disintegration of romantic and modernist dogma in ironic versions of that most characteristic of romantic literary forms, the *Künstlerroman*. Where the traditional Künstlerroman had dramatized the success of the artist as artist, in Thomas Mann's *Death in Venice*, or Joyce's *Portrait of the Artist as a Young Man*, for example, these latterday instances of the genre, like Camus's *The Plague* or Herman Broch's *Death of Vergil*, gave the standard plot a negative twist, showing the increasing difficulty, in some cases impossibility, of writing meaningfully in the changed social circumstances of the postwar world.

Norman Mailer in *Of a Fire on the Moon* portrayed the first landing on the moon in 1969 as an assault by science on humanistic literature and the arts, preempting the god of poetry, Apollo, for the name of the mission, and transforming the traditional symbol of the romantic imagination, the moon, into a lifeless scientific object. The overwhelming achievements of the scientific approach to knowledge were making it impossible for writers like Mailer any longer to claim that literature offered much understanding, or was even useful in any way. He dramatized this loss of artistic confidence by showing that before the mighty power of science it became nearly impossible for the writer Aquarius-Mailer to write his novel asserting the truths known to the imagination. The Manson family in California, the drugged youth at Woodstock, Teddy Kennedy at Chappaquidick, once Mailer's allies in the radical left, all failed the liberal-romantic cause in the fateful summer of 1969. The artist alone was left to defend the imaginative and the vital against the assaults of science with his novel. But he is too demoralized to fight back in the manner of Byron or Hugo, and the best he can do is to produce, with great heavings and gruntings, a tangled "factive" composite of NASA press releases, autobiographical fragments, reports of the moon shot for *Esquire*, a great deal of self-analysis, technologese, and some rambling philosophizing asserting that the landing of men on the moon was probably a good thing in the long run for humankind.

Bernard Malamud in *The Tenants* (1971) set the scene of writing in a decayed New York tenement where all the ugliness and race hatred and misgovernment and money-grubbing of the twentieth century meet. There, in a murderous competition, a black and a Jewish writer seek obsessively, each isolated from the other, to find *les mots justes* and achieve the Flaubertian perfect work of art, in the belief that their art can change the ugliness and hatred of the world to beauty and love. It is not just a matter of the literary work of art persuading the world to love and to cherish beauty but more that, in high romantic fashion, the presence in the world of the artwork embodying love and beauty will give those qualities a mysterious reality. There are some futile attempts to teach one another what they know, the black his furious energy and indignation, the Jew his learning and verbal skills, but they achieve only more hatred. The tenement in which they live becomes more and more uninhabitable, haunted by all the nightmares of modern urban life, and they at last destroy each other's work. In the end, still trying to write about love and justice, they kill each other. Their unfinished works, fluttering yellow sheets of paper, go out with the garbage, leaving the world they had tried to change slightly the worse for their efforts.

Nabokov's *Pale Fire* (1962) locates the literary scene in the modern university—*Wordsmith*, a parody of Cornell, where Nabokov unwillingly taught for a time until released by the *Lolita* royalties—where the university system, particularly scholarship and criticism, pervert literature in bizarre ways. A totally academicized poet, John Shade, produces an autobiographical poem, "Pale Fire," which is a collage of all Western literature: obscure quotations, like the title from Shakespeare's *Timon of Athens,* Pope's couplets, Wordsworth's plot of the growth of a poet's mind, conversational tones lifted from T. S. Eliot, a wheelbarrow from William Carlos Williams, and on and on. After Shade's death, his critic-professor-reader, Charles Kinbote, lecturer in Zemblan, who displays considerable signs of madness, produces a long edition of "Pale Fire" with elaborate scholarly apparatus, particularly extensive explanatory notes, in order to make a scholarly reputation and achieve tenure. Unfortunately, the scholarship is bogus and the commentary has nothing to do with Shade's life and poem, everything to do with some personal fantasy of Kinbote's about being the deposed king of a Graustarkian central European country, which he loads on the back of the poem via the notes. It is never made absolutely clear whether Kinbote's story is delusion or fact, or whether it makes any difference. *Pale Fire* is on the surface a grotesque parody of the modern university and its destructive effects on literary art, but underneath this satire the novel is grappling with a growing narcissism and solipsism in modern life that are making any kind of communication, including the privileged literary kind between authors and readers, increasingly difficult, perhaps ultimately impossible.

In Saul Bellow's *Humboldt's Gift* (1973) the indifference of the modern public and the growing feeling that the writer has nothing to say silences and eventually kills a poet modeled on Delmore Schwartz. Von Humboldt Fleischer, born on the IRT and named after a statue his mother saw in the park, is the romantic poet in a latter age where he has become a buffoon to himself and others. The sacred words for him are still the keywords of romanticism, "Poetry, Beauty, Love, Waste Land, Alienation, Politics, History, The Unconscious," always capitalized. But he fritters his talent and his life away playing out the role of poète maudit, never getting around to writing anything very serious because always a poet in residence somewhere, applying for a foundation grant, writing articles for various little magazines, drinking, gossiping, taking drugs. As Humboldt himself puts it after buying a big car, he is "the first poet with power brakes." In the end the gift he leaves to the world and to his friend, Bellow-Citrine, a writer of serviceable prose, is a bizarre, mocking movie script, which makes a lot of money.

Our storytellers, by now prose writers all, in their characteristic way, made up humanistic stories about the way literary people, particularly poets and novelists, found themselves in new and unanticipated circumstances that, in enormously painful and frustrating ways, were squeezing literature out of the social world. Mailer's persona, the writer Aquarius, speaks for all these belated artists when he is forced to acknowledge the power of science and technology in the launching of the mighty rocket, Apollo 11, "the world had changed, even as he had thought to be pushing on it with *his* mighty ego. And it had changed in ways he did not recognize, had never anticipated, and could possibly not comprehend now. The change was mightier than he had counted on."

NASA and the Apollo mission, an abandoned tenement in the Bronx, Wordsmith University, the New York intellectual scene—these are striking images of a changed world in which literature as it has been understood in the romantic and modern eras no longer can function, no longer has a place, in the end ceases to exist.

Literary criticism recognized the death of literature in the abstract terms of reception aesthetics, hermeneutics, structuralism, deconstruction, feminism, and Foucauldian Marxism. And in the day-to-day world, in ways I have earlier tried to show, literature got fatally tangled up with classrooms and courtrooms, technological change from print to electronics, dictionary decisions about the nature of verbal authority, quarrels over copyright. In these places the voices carry the ominous note:

> "What do they mean by 'letters' and 'literature' apart from language? I suppose . . . they want 'chatter about Shelley.' I told them that we did not want to discuss Harriet, having enough to do with Helen, Theodora, and Mary Stewart."

> "Will you tell us as an expert in English literature what are the matters which ought to be taken into account in assessing the literary merits of a book?"—"I think that's a very difficult thing to do in general terms, and I think it varies very much with the kind of book it is. We are here discussing a novel, and I think one of the things one would wish to take into account is whether it is a true and sincere representation of an aspect of life. . . . the book is concerned with a very important situation; it is concerned with the relations of men and women, with their sexual relations, with the nature of marriage, and these are all matters of deep importance to all of us."

> "What is plagiarism, apart from legal questions of ownership, copyright or financial gain? How, for example, does it differ from repetition, reportage, quotation, paraphrase, exposition and other ways of reproducing previously existing material? Plagiarism is closer to pride, a sin of the spirit, than to the criminal activities of the burglar."

> "A bitter line of hostility to civilization . . . runs through modern literature." "Shut the motherfucker down!" "Off the Pigs." "The nightstick of verification and the handcuffs of validity." "The idea that the Truth is One—unambiguous, self-consistent, and knowable [is one of] the murderous fictions of our history." "To write well is counterrevolutionary."

> "[The new Cambridge Lawrence is an] interesting departure from the normal run of scholarly editions in that it is indissolubly linked with the copyright of the main works themselves."

"That statement is no longer operative."

"Napoleon and Lincoln had to achieve fame the old-fashioned way by conquering Europe and freeing the slaves. Celebrity can be created on demand."

"The literary dimensions of language [are] largely obscured if one submits uncritically to the authority of reference," "the myth of semantic correspondence between sign and referent." "On voit donc qu'une solution du problème juif qui viserait à la création d'une colonie juive isolée de l'Europe, n'entraînerait pas, pour la vie littéraire de l'Occident, de conséquences déplorables."

In this modern babel, the old literature of romanticism and modernism died, partly by suicide, partly by felonious assault. The temptation to blame particular people or particular groups is strong. There is, as usual, more than enough blame to go around, for both the old order and the new used literature more often in the very human way of furthering their own personal ends than in any really serious pursuit of knowledge. Tempting, too, to fasten blame on particular changes in social life such as television watching or breakdowns in literacy, or even to single out various new technologies such as the electronic constellation that is replacing print as the primary mode of communication. But the very number of people and things that have affected literature suggests that the death of the old literature has to be understood not as a culpable act but as part of a broad cultural change.

Deconstruction and television, to compare small things to great in their cultural effect, are, for all of their heavy impact on the old literature and its sustaining beliefs, only two aspects of a recent social shift that has registered very high on the scale of cultural disturbances. The death of the old literature has itself been only one part, and a relatively small one, of an extensive social disorientation that has in the past thirty years broken up a large number of our traditional institutions and value systems. There is as yet no satisfactory name for this extensive social shift, terms like *postindustrialism* and *post-*

modernism recording only our sense that particular ways of life have passed without specifying what has replaced them. But that a big change has come, whether by evolution or revolution, I think few would dispute.

Although we may not be able yet to say what wonders have been wrought, we know the numerous symptoms of what has happened: a shift to a service from a manufacturing economy, from a print to an electronic mode of information storage and retrieval, from an economics of scarcity and saving to the "affluent society" of consumers, from a politics of representation to one of individual and group social activism, from a positivist conception of fact to a relativist conception of "image," from an acceptance of authority to individual freedom of choice, and from disciplined self-denial to hedonism, permissiveness, and self-indulgence, the cult of narcissism. Some of these cultural tendencies are, of course, outright shams that will not long endure, and others probably have little long-run social usefulness, but all are part of a trend showing very distinctly the direction in which Western society, perhaps Eastern as well, has been going for some time.

Seen in this context it was inevitable that the old literature, like one of the industrial cities of the rustbelt, should also have collapsed in this time of fundamental change. And with literature, as with other social institutions in the postindustrial society, it is by no means clear as yet what form it will assume in the future. There is always the possibility that literature was so much a product of print culture and industrial capitalism, as bardic poetry and heroic epic were of tribal oral society, that, like chivalry in the age of gunpowder, it will simply disappear in the electronic age, or dwindle to a merely ceremonial role, something like Peking opera perhaps. The assemblage and institutionalization of the texts, beliefs, and practices that constitute literature was, after all, a historical event, and there is no reason why it should not join many other cultural institutions in history's dream-dump. The texts that form the substantial center of literature will be

eagerly reclaimed by classics as a part of classical civilization, absorbed into the history of various languages and nationalities and
reprocessed for evidence in various types of sociological, psychological,
and religious studies.

There still is, however, considerable energy in the idea of literature
as a distinct way of writing and thinking, and the more advanced
literary people of our time, accepting that the old literature is gone,
strongly assert that they have already created a new conception of
literature and assigned it a new social role. Deconstruction in this view
cleared the ground of the pretensions of the old romantic and modern
literature to express permanent and universal human truths in monumental form by means of some gnostic power of the imagination. At
the same time deconstruction provided the needed theoretical underpinnings for a new literature by exposing the strategies used by various
ideologies to create the appearance of "truth" in the interests of gaining
power and exercising hegemony over others. Literature as enabled by
this kind of awareness that there is nothing outside the text is thought
to encourage the free play of interpretation and further the construction
of "truths" that nourish life. Feminism, black studies, Chicano power,
ethnic literatures, gay liberation, new historicists, and various Marxist
groups like the British cultural materialists are free in the brave new
world to use literature as one means of furthering not only their own
social programs but the more rad-lib causes of openness, toleration,
relativisim, individualism, freedom, and experimentation. English literary cultural materialism, for example, defines its program as a "commitment to the transformation of a social order that exploits people on
grounds of race, gender, sexuality and class" (Holderness).

But the attractiveness of these social programs—feminism's bright
opportunity, for example, to march in the liberation of women from
ancient bondage—is bought, it is important to notice, by heavily discounting the texts that are the capital endowment of literature. It is
not, I want to stress, that these ways of reading literature, if partial,

are inaccurate. The old literature was itself thoroughly politicized in ways I have described in chapter 1, and there is no question that it often treated women in at times a contemptuous, nearly always a patronizing fashion. My problem with the new approaches is not their accuracy or fairness, only their usefulness in maintaining and preserving the works of literature, or the "texts" if that term is preferable, on which the entire literary enterprise, past and present, depend. Whatever else literature has been and may become in the future, its own prosperity and its social usefulness rely on a group of poems, plays, novels that are by general agreement not only its principal stock in trade but its accumulated capital as well. Give away, lose, or discredit these texts—Homer, Shakespeare, Balzac—and literature is out of business. The commercial metaphors are intentional, for we are talking not about some metaphysical properties but about literature's function and existence in a give and take society. Take away the works that are still for the moment agreed to be literature, and what is left? Only a hodgepodge of institutional odds and ends without a center, a decaying instructional system, a set of professional arrangements, a library category, a high-culture avant-garde art circle, a few publishers and reviewers, a few passing political and social causes.

But this is precisely what the more radical critics have been doing. Deconstructors show the emptiness of literary language and texts, Marxists show how the works of literature have been used as the instruments of power to establish the ideology of one or another dominant class—"Shakespeare as a Hegemonic Instrument"—while feminists demonstrate literature's use in the past wrongfully to suppress the female. In this way literature has been being emptied out in the service of social and political causes that are considered more important than the texts themselves, to which the texts are, in fact, only means to a greater end. The literary text has no meaning, or, what comes to the same thing, it has as many and whatever meanings anyone wants to find in it. It has lied in numerous ways to serve the authority of class and state. It has been the instrument of oppression, furthering imperialism and colonialism, establishing male hegemony, suppressing any movement toward freedom from authority. There is political shock value in these assaults upon the integrity of the text, but it is difficult to see how in the long run literature that has been stripped of any positive value can be considered worth reading and interpreting.

It may well be more realistic to see all these radical types of criticism that have discredited the literary texts as the last apocalyptic phases of an old literary order collapsing in on itself in a time of radical change, rather than as the bringers of a new more free and open literature. It has often been suggested that for all their appearance of being new, the radical criticisms of recent years are in fact only hypertrophied extensions of old literary values. Deconstruction, for example, with its microscopically close readings of the text and its emphasis on total irony is obviously a development of the old formalistic modes of literary interpretation such as aestheticism or the new criticism. Indeterminacy is an extreme form of what Keats called "negative capability," and a version of the seven types of ambiguity Empson defined for the new criticism. Literary neo-Marxism with its uncompromising and relentless attacks on the main line of modern civilization closely resembles traditional romantic reaction, as in the followers of F. R. Leavis, for example, against industrial society. But where literature was earlier privileged as an exception, it is now included among the corrupt institutions of capitalism. The last phase of the old romantic and modern literature rather than ending in the 1960s may have extended to a last apocalyptic period in which the angels of death were not visitants from some other world but exaggerated versions of positions which, positive in their earlier forms, became destructive in their extremes. The beginnings of a new literature would then appear, if at all, only when some new way, plausible and positive, is voiced to claim for the traditional literary works a place of some importance and usefulness in individual life and for society as a whole.

Works Cited

(Works available in standard editions, such as Boswell's *Life of Johnson*, Wordsworth's preface to the *Lyrical Ballads*, or Diderot's *Encyclopédie*, are not listed.)

Aarsleff, Hans. *From Locke to Saussure: Essays on the Study of Language*. Minneapolis, 1982.

Abrams, Meyer. *The Mirror and the Lamp: Romantic Theory and the Critical Tradition*. New York, 1953.

Adams, Hazard. *Critical Theory since Plato*. New York, 1971.

Adelman, Clifford. "On the Paper Trail of the Class of '72." *New York Times*, July 22, 1989, A25.

Arac, Jonathan. "History and Mystery: The Criticism of Frank Kermode." *Salamagundi* 55 (1982).

Barthes, Roland. "The Death of the Author." *Image, Music, Text*. Trans. Stephen Heath. Glasgow, 1977.

Belanger, Terry. "Publishers and Writers in Eighteenth-Century England." *Books and Their Readers in Eighteenth-Century England*. Ed. Isabel Rivers. London, 1982.

Bell, Daniel. *The Coming of Post-Industrial Society*. New York, 1974.

Belsey, Catherine. "Re-reading the Great Tradition." In Widdowson.

Benjamin, Walter. "The Work of Art in the Age of Mechanical Reproduction." In *Illuminations*. Ed. Hannah Arendt, trans. Harry Zohn. New York, 1969, 217.

Biederman, Susan Duke. "Art Laws Don't Protect Films from Alteration." *New York Times*, December 11, 1986, Op-Ed page.

Blackmur, R. P. "A Critic's Job of Work" (1935). In Adams.

Bloom, Allan. *The Closing of the American Mind.* New York, 1987.

Bloom, Harold. *The Anxiety of Influence.* New York, 1975.

————. See "Plagiarism—A Symposium."

Boorstin, Daniel J. *The Image: A Guide to Pseudo-Events in America.* New York, 1962.

Booth, Wayne. *Critical Understanding: The Powers and Limits of Pluralism.* Chicago, 1979.

Brooks, Cleanth, and W. K. Wimsatt, Jr. *Literary Criticism: A Short History.* New York, 1957.

Brooks, David. "From Western Lit to Westerns as Lit." *Wall Street Journal,* February 27, 1988.

Brustein, Robert. "Don't Punish the Arts." In "Dialogue, Art and the Taxpayers Money." *New York Times,* June 23, 1989, A29.

Burnham, Sophie. "As the Stakes in the Art World Rise, So Do Laws and Lawsuits." *New York Times,* February 15, 1987, 2:1.

Carnegie Foundation for the Advancement of Teaching. "The Condition of the Professoriate: Attitudes and Trends, 1989." Princeton, 1989.

Chadwick, Hector Munro, and Norah (Kershaw). *The Growth of Literature.* 3 vols. Cambridge, 1932–40.

Chapin, Schuyler, and Alberta Arthurs. "A Bill of Rights for the Arts." *New York Times,* October 29, 1987, Op-Ed page.

Cheney, Lynne V. *Humanities in America: Report to the President, the Congress, and the American People.* National Endowment for the Humanities, Washington, D.C. September 12, 1988.

Chesterfield, Philip Dormer Stanhope, Earl of. "The Language of Ladies." *The World,* 101, December 5, 1754.

Collins, John Churton. *The Study of English Literature: A Plea for Its Recognition and Organization at the Universities.* London, 1891.

Corngold, Stanley. *TLS,* November 11, 1988, Letters.

Culler, Jonathan. *Structuralist Poetics, Structuralism, Linguistics and the Study of Literature.* London, 1975.

Darnton, Robert. "First Steps towards a History of Reading." *Australian Journal of French Studies* 22 (1986), 5.

————. "Philosophers Trim the Tree of Knowledge: The Epistemological Strategy of the *Encyclopédie*." In Robert Darnton, *The Great Cat Massacre and Other Episodes in French Cultural History*. New York, 1985.

De Man, Paul. *Paul de Man: Wartime Journalism, 1939–1943*. Ed. Werner Hamacher, Neil Hertz, and Thomas Keenan. Lincoln, Neb., 1988.

————. "Semiology and Rhetoric." In *Textual Strategies: Perspectives in Post-Structuralist Criticism*. Ed. Josué V. Harari. Ithaca, 1979, 121.

DeMaria, Robert, Jr. *Johnson's Dictionary and the Language of Learning*. Chapel Hill, 1986.

————. "The Politics of Johnson's *Dictionary*." *PMLA*, January 1989, 64.

Derrida, Jacques. "Like the Sound of the Deep Sea within a Shell: Paul de Man's War." Trans. Peggy Kamuf. *Critical Inquiry* 14 (1988), 639.

————. "Structure, Sign and Play." In *The Structuralist Controversy*. Ed. Richard Macksey and Eugenio Donato. Baltimore, 1970, 147.

Dictionary of American Regional English. Frederic G. Cassidy, chief ed. Cambridge, Mass., 1985–.

Dilthey, Wilhelm. *Gesämmelte Schriften*. 19 vols. Leipzig and Göttingen, 1914–82.

Dullea, Georgia. "City Makes It Official: They're Artists." *New York Times*, October 21, 1986, B1.

Dunlap, David W. "Judge Upholds Effort to Move Sculpture." *New York Times*, September 1, 1987, B1.

————. "Moving Day Arrives for Disputed Sculpture." *New York Times*, March 11, 1989, A29.

Eagleton, Terry. "Escape into the Ineffable." *TLS*, November 24–30, 1989, 1,291.

————. *Literary Theory: An Introduction*. Oxford, 1983.

Eighteenth-Century Short Title Catalogue, the British Library Collections. Ed. R. C. Alston and M. J. Crump. 113 fiches, later on disks. British Library, London, 1984.

Eisenstein, Elizabeth. *The Printing Press as an Agent of Change*. 2 vols. Cambridge, 1979.

Eliot, T. S. "The Function of Criticism." *Selected Essays, 1917–1932*. New York, 1932.

————. "The Social Function of Poetry." In T. S. Eliot, *On Poetry and Poets*. New York, 1957.

————. "Tradition and the Individual Talent." In *Selected Essays, 1917–1932*. New York, 1932.

Englesing, R. "Die Perioden der Lesergeschichte in der Neuzeit: Das statische Ausmass und die sociokulturelle Bedeutung dere Lektüre." In *Archiv für Geschichte des Buchwesens* 10 (1969), cols. 944–1002.

Febvre, Lucien, and Henri-Jean Martin. *The Coming of the Book: The Impact of Printing, 1450–1800*. Trans. David Gerard. London, 1976.

Fenton, James. *TLS*, April 2, 1982, Letters.

Fischer, Michael. *Does Deconstruction Make Any Difference?* Bloomington, 1985.

Fish, Stanley. *Is There a Text in This Class?* Cambridge, Mass., 1980.

Flaubert, Gustave. *Selected Letters*. Trans. Francis Steegmuller. London, 1954.

Foucault, Michel. "What Is an Author?" In *Textual Strategies: Perspectives in Post-Structuralist Criticism*. Ed. Josué V. Harari. Ithaca, 1979, 141.

Freedman, Samuel G. "Actors Equity Protests Beckett Cast Criticism." *New York Times*, January 9, 1985, C17.

Freeman, Edward Augustus. *The Life and Letters of Edward A. Freeman*. Ed. W. R. W. Stephens, 2 vols. London, 1895.

Frost, David. "The White Hotel." *TLS*, April 9, 1982, Letters.

Frye, Northrop. *Anatomy of Criticism*. Princeton, 1957.

Goodman, Lord. See "Plagiarism—A Symposium."

Goody, Jack. *Literacy in Traditional Societies*. Cambridge, 1968.

Gorman, Robert A. "Copyright and the Professoriate: A Primer and Some Recent Developments." *Academe* (September–October 1987), 29.

Graff, Gerald. "Looking Past the de Man Case." In Hamacher, Hertz, and Keenan, *Responses*, 246.

————. *Professing Literature: An Institutional History*. Chicago, 1987.

Graff, Gerald, and William E. Cain. "Peace Plan for the Canon Wars." *Nation*, March 6, 1989, 310.

Hamacher, Werner, Neil Hertz, and Thomas Keenan, eds. *Paul de Man: Wartime Journalism, 1939–1943*. Lincoln, Neb., 1988.

————. *Responses on Paul de Man's Wartime Journalism*. Lincoln, Neb., 1989.

Harris, Neil. "Who Owns Our Myths? Heroism and Copyright in an Age of Mass Culture." *Social Research* 52 (1985), 243.

Harris, Roy. "The History Men." *TLS*, September 3, 1982, 935.

————. *Landmarks in Linguistic Thought: The Western Tradition from Socrates to Saussure*. New York, 1989.

Hartman, Geoffrey. *Criticism in the Wilderness*. New Haven, 1980.

Havelock, Eric A. *A Preface to Plato*. Cambridge, Mass., 1963.

Hill, Geoffrey. "Common Weal, Common Woe." *TLS*, April 21, 1989, 411.

Hirsch, E. Donald, Jr. "What Isn't Literature?" In *What Is Literature?* Ed. George Hernadi. Bloomington, 1978.

————. *Cultural Literacy: What Every American Needs to Know*. Boston, 1987.

Holderness, Graham, ed. *The Shakespeare Myth*. Manchester, 1989.

Holroyd, Michael, and Sandra Jobson. "Copyrights and Wrongs: D. H. Lawrence." *TLS*, September 3, 1982, 943.

Horowitz, Irving Louis. *The Crisis of Publishing in a Post-Industrial Society*. New York, 1987.

Hudson, Liam. "Recalling a Scapegoat." *TLS*, November 3–9, 1989, 1201.

Hunter, Ian. *Culture and Government: The Emergence of Literary Education*. London, 1989.

Jakobson, Roman. *Language in Literature*. Cambridge, Mass., 1987.

James, Henry. *The Art of Fiction*. In Adams.

Jameson, Fredric. *The Political Unconscious: Narrative as a Socially Symbolic Act*. Ithaca, 1981.

Johnson, Kirk. "In Connecticut, Debate over Art for Captive Audience." *New York Times*, March 25, 1989, C29.

Kantaris, Sylvia. "The White Hotel." *TLS*, April 23, 1982, Letters.

Kaplan, James. "Inside the Club." *New York Times Magazine*, June 11, 1989, 62.

Kaplan, Justin. *An Unhurried View of Copyright*. New York, 1967.

Katsh, Ethan. *The Electronic Media and the Transformation of Law.* New York, 1989.

Kenrick, D. A. "The White Hotel." *TLS*, March 26, 1982, Letters.

Kernan, Alvin. *The Imaginary Library: An Essay on Literature and Society.* Princeton, 1982.

———. *Samuel Johnson and the Impact of Print.* Princeton, 1989. (Originally *Printing Technology, Letters, and Samuel Johnson.* Princeton, 1987.)

Kingson, Jennifer A. "Where Information Is All, Pleas Arise for Less of It." *New York Times*, July 9, 1989, E9.

Kozol, Jonathan. *Illiterate America.* New York, 1985.

Kristeller, Paul O. "The Modern System of the Arts." In *Renaissance Thought.* Vol. 2. New York, 1965, 163.

Kula, Witold. *Measures and Men.* Trans. R. Szreter. Princeton, 1986.

Lacey, Dan. "Publishing and the New Technology." In *Books, Libraries and Electronics: Essays on the Future of Written Communications.* Foreword by Carol A. Nermeyer. White Plains, N.Y., 1982.

Landes, David S. *Revolution in Time: Clocks and the Making of the Modern World.* Cambridge, Mass., 1983.

Leavis, F. R. *The Common Pursuit.* London, 1952.

Lehmann-Haupt, Christopher. "William Burroughs." *New York Times*, October 31, 1988, C20.

Levine, George, and others. *Speaking for the Humanities.* American Council of Learned Societies, Occasional Paper 7. New York, 1989.

Lévi-Strauss, Claude. *La pensée sauvage.* Paris, 1962.

Lippmann, Walter. *Public Opinion.* New York, 1922.

Lovejoy, Arthur O. *The Great Chain of Being: A Study of the History of an Idea.* New York, 1960.

Lubasch, Arnold H. "Salinger Biography Is Blocked." *New York Times*, January 30, 1987, A1.

Macdonald, Dwight. *Against the American Grain.* New York, 1962.

McEwan, Ian. See "Plagiarism—A Symposium."

McGill, Douglas C. "Tilted Arc." *New York Times*, January 30, 1987.

Mack, Maynard. *Prose and Cons: Monologues on Several Occasions.* New Haven, privately printed, 1989.

McLuhan, Marshall. *The Gutenberg Galaxy.* Toronto, 1962.

Mallon, Thomas. *Stolen Words: Forays into the Origins and Ravages of Plagiarism.* New York, 1989.

Mehrabian, Albert. *Silent Messages.* Belmont, Calif., 1971.

Mellers, Wilfrid. See "Plagiarism—A Symposium."

Meyrowitz, Joshua. *No Sense of Place: The Impact of Electronic Media on Social Behavior.* New York, 1985.

Mitchell, C. J. "The Spread and Fluctuation of Eighteenth-Century Printing." *Studies in Voltaire and the Eighteenth Century* 230 (1985), 305.

Mitgang, Herbert. "Ramifications of Literary Lawsuits: The 'Bell Jar' and Salinger Cases." *New York Times,* February 3, 1987.

Morley, John. In Collins.

Morris, William. *How I Became a Socialist.* London, 1986.

Murray, K. M. Elisabeth. *Caught in the Web of Words: James H. Murray and the OED.* New Haven, 1977.

Ohman, Richard. *English in America.* New York, 1976.

Oman, Ralph. "Black and White and Red All Over." *New York Times,* June 24, 1987, Op-Ed page.

Ong, Walter J. *Orality and Literacy: The Technologizing of the Word.* London, 1982.

———. "Samuel Johnson and the Printed Word." *Review* (Fall 1988), 97.

Palmer, D. J. *The Rise of English Studies.* New York, 1965.

Parsons, Ian. "Copyright and Society." In *Essays in the History of Publishing.* Ed. Asa Briggs. London, 1974, 29.

"Plagiarism—A Symposium." *TLS,* April 9, 1982.

Podhoretz, Norman. *Breaking Ranks: A Political Memoir.* New York, 1979.

Pool, I. de S. *The Social Impact of the Telephone.* Cambridge, Mass., 1977.

Poster, Mark. *Foucault, Marxism and History: Mode of Production versus Mode of Information.* Oxford, 1984.

Quine, W. V. *Theories and Things.* Cambridge, Mass., 1981.

Raleigh, Sir Walter Alexander. *A Selection from the Letters of Sir Walter Raleigh (1880–1922).* Ed. Lady Raleigh, Preface by David Nichol Smith. London, 1928.

Rank, Hugh, ed. *Language and Public Policy*. Urbana, 1971.

Rein, Irving, Philip Kotler, and Martin R. Stoller. *High Visibility*. New York, 1987.

Rickman, H. P. *Meaning in History: W. Dilthey's Thoughts on History and Society*. London, 1961.

Rolph, C. H. *The Trial of Lady Chatterley: Regina v. Penguin Books Ltd.* Harmondsworth, 1961.

Rose, Mark. "The Author as Proprietor: *Donaldson v. Beckett* and the Genealogy of Modern Authorship." *Representations* 23 (1988), 51.

Rotman, Brian. "Life since God." *TLS*, April 7, 1989, 373.

Ruskin, John. *The Stones of Venice*. Vol. 2. London, 1899, 6, 165.

Ryan, Michael. "Self Evidence." *Diacritics* 10 (1980).

Scanlan, Margaret. *Traces of Another Time: History and Politics in Postwar British Fiction*. Princeton, 1990.

Schäfer, Jurgen. *Documentation in the O.E.D.* Oxford, 1980.

Schwartz, Lawrence H. *Creating Faulkner's Reputation: The Politics of Modern Literary Criticism*. Knoxville, Tenn., 1988.

Solotaroff, Ted. "The Literary-Industrial Complex." *New Republic*, June 8, 1987, 28.

Sontag, Susan. "Against Interpretation." In Adams.

Sparrow, John. "Regina v. Penguin Books Ltd.: An Undisclosed Element in the Case." *Encounter* 101 (February 1962), 35.

Stange, E. "Millions of Books Are Turning to Dust—Can They Be Saved?" *New York Times Book Review*, March 29, 1987, 3.

Steiner, George. *After Babel*. London, 1975.

———. "Books in an Age of Post-Literacy." *Publishers' Weekly*, May 24, 1985, 44.

———. "Future Literacies." In *Bluebeard's Castle*. New Haven, 1971.

———. *The Language of Silence*. New York, 1967.

"Simon and Schuster Sues over Son of Sam Law." *New York Times*, August 6, 1987, C24.

Sutherland, John. See "Plagiarism—A Symposium."

Taylor, Stuart, Jr. "Court Backs 'Propaganda' Label for Three Canadian Films." *New York Times*, April 29, 1987, A28.

Tennant, Emma. "The White Hotel." *TLS*, April 9, 1982, Letters.

Thomas, D. M. "The White Hotel." *TLS*, April 2, 1982, Letters.

Tompkins, Jane P. "The Reader in History: The Changing Shape of Literary Response." In *Reader-Response Criticism: From Formalism to Post-Structuralism*. Ed. Jane P. Tompkins. Baltimore, 1980, 201.

Trilling, Lionel. *Beyond Culture*. Harmondsworth, 1967.

Trithemius, John (1462–1516). *In Praise of Scribes*. Ed. Klaus Arnold, trans. Roland Behrendt. Lawrence, Kans., 1974.

Urmson, J. O. See "Plagiarism—A Symposium."

U.S. Government. Bureau of the Census. *Historical Statistics of the United States: Colonial Times to 1970*. Washington, D.C., 1975, p. 808.

————. *Statistical Abstracts of the United States, 1984*. Washington, D.C., 1985, p. 236.

U.S. Government. Department of Education, Office of Educational Research and Improvement, Center for Education Statistics. *Digest of Education Statistics, 1987*. Washington, D.C., 1987, table 74.

Valéry, Paul. *Aesthetics*. Trans. Ralph Manheim. New York, 1964.

Vidal, Gore. *Matters of Fact and of Fiction: Essays, 1973–1976*. New York, 1977.

Vincent, David. *Literary and Popular Culture: England, 1750–1914*. Cambridge, 1989.

Walker, Gay, Jane Greenfield, John Fox, and Jeffrey S. Simonoff. "The Yale Survey: A Large-Scale Study of Book Deterioration in the Yale University Library." College and Research Libraries publication 46 (1985), 111.

Wellek, René. "Literary Criticism and Philosophy." *Scrutiny* 6 (March 1937–38), 376.

————. "What Is Literature?" In *What Is Literature?* Ed. Paul Hernadi. Bloomington, 1978.

Wellek, René, and Austin Warren. *Theory of Literature*. New York, 1956.

Whitby, Max. "The Instant Archive." *TLS*, October 16, 1987, 1138.

Widdowson, Peter, ed. *Re-Reading English*. London, 1982.

Williams, Raymond. *Communications*. New York, 1976.

————. *Culture and Society, 1780–1950*. London, 1958.

————. *Keywords: A Vocabulary of Culture and Society*. New York, 1970.

Wimsatt, W. K., Jr. "Battering the Object: The Ontological Appoach." In *Contemporary Criticism*. Stratford-Upon-Avon Studies, 12. London, 1970, 61.

————. "Johnson's Dictionary." In *New Light on Dr. Johnson*. Ed. F. W. Hilles. New Haven, 1959, 65.

Woodmansee, Martha. "The Genius of Copyright: Economic and Legal Conditions of the Emergence of the Author." *Eighteenth-Century Studies* 4 (1984), 425.

Woolf, Virginia. "Mr. Bennett and Mrs. Brown" (1924). In *The Common Reader*. London, 1925.

Yale University Council Committee on the Library. Unpublished report of May 1987.

Index

Satire – 88–9